HIKE
THE CHANNEL ISLANDS

Hike. Contemplate what makes you happy and what makes you happier still. Follow a trail or blaze a new one. **Hike**. Think about what you can do to expand your life and someone else's. **Hike**. Slow down. Gear up. **Hike**. Connect with friends. Re-connect with nature.

Hike. Shed stress. Feel blessed. **Hike** to remember. **Hike** to forget. **Hike** for recovery. **Hike** for discovery. **Hike**. Enjoy the beauty of providence. **Hike**. Share the way, The Hiker's Way, on the long and winding trail we call life.

HIKE
THE CHANNEL
ISLANDS

BY
JOHN MCKINNEY
& CHUCK GRAHAM

TheTrailmaster.com

HIKE the Channel Islands, Best Day Hikes in Channel Islands National Park by John McKinney and Chuck Graham

HIKE the Channel Islands ©2022 The Trailmaster, Inc.

ISBN: 978-0934161-93-0

Book Design by Lisa DeSpain
Cartography by Mark Chumley
Cover photos by Chuck Graham
HIKE Series Editor: Cheri Rae
PHOTO CREDITS: Courtesy National Park Service, p. 21; Holli Harmon painting, p. 127; All other photos by Chuck Graham.

Published by Olympus Press and The Trailmaster, Inc.
TheTrailmaster.com (Visit our site for a complete listing of all Trailmaster publications, products, and services.) Although The Trailmaster, Inc. and the author have made every attempt to ensure that information in this book is accurate, they are not responsible for any loss, damage, injury, or inconvenience that may occur to you while using this information. You are responsible for your own safety; the fact that an activity or trail is described in this book does not mean it will be safe for you. Trail conditions can change from day to day; always check local conditions and know your limitations.

CONTENTS

I Anacapa Island

Easy to reach, impossible to forget. Start your love
affair with the Channel Islands with a hike around
Anacapa

II Santa Cruz Island

From Scorpion Anchorage

For first timers to the isle, an ideal intro, complete with
clifftop trails and postcard-perfect harbor

Semi-tough loop trail featuring the island scrub jay,
stellar vistas and a curious oil well

Tackle the highest summit within park boundaries on a
challenging new loop trail

III Santa Rosa Island

IV San Miguel Island

V Santa Barbara Island

The "Inspiration Point" on Anacapa
is one of the many inspiring overlooks on the islands
that beckon the adventurous hiker.

EVERY TRAIL TELLS A STORY.

INTRODUCTION

With its sheer, honeycombed cliffs, wave-battered sea caves, stream-fed canyons, windswept beaches and cobbled coves, Channel Islands National Park is a unique place to roam. When the mainland is obscured by fog, as it often is, it can seem to the hiker that this windswept archipelago is as far away as the Hawaiian Islands.

Channel Islands National Park is sometimes referred to as "the Galapagos Islands of the north." Top priority is given to protecting seals and sea lions, endemic flora and fauna, fragile archaeological sites, and what might be the final resting place of Portuguese navigator Juan Rodriguez Cabrillo, who explored the California coast for the Spanish crown in the 16th century.

Each of the islands has a special draw. Anacapa is the most accessible and offers the visitor a sampling of the charms of the larger islands to the west. Santa Cruz is California's largest island and boasts the most varied coastline and topography as well as the highest peak (2,434 feet) and tranquil natural harbors.

Santa Rosa Island has an extensive archaeological record; scientists believe the island was inhabited at least 13,000 years ago. San Miguel Island hosts 30,000 or more seals and sea lions during mating season and what may be the largest pinniped colony on earth. Tiny and remote Santa Barbara Island is prized by those visitors determined to visit each and every one of the isles in Channel Islands National Park.

What never ceases to amaze us, even after a combined 60-plus years of hiking the Channel Islands, are the views back to the mainland. It's a strange feeling indeed to be immersed in the natural beauty of the islands knowing the Los Angeles megalopolis, the nation's second largest city and home to 10 million people, is located just 60 miles away to the east.

While one of the most magnificent national parks in the U.S., Channel Islands remains one of its least known and visited. More than 300 thousand visitors a year drop by the national park visitor center in Ventura; however, only ten percent of them venture out to the islands. About 30 thousand visitors per year set foot on the islands.

Santa Cruz Island, the main hiker's hub of Channel Islands National Park, is four times the size of Manhattan Island. At last count, Manhattan had a population of 1.6 million while Santa Cruz Island had zero permanent residents.

On many hikes, such as the Montañon Ridge Loop Trail on Santa Cruz Island and the hike out to East Point on Santa Rosa Island, it's rare to meet another hiker. More likely you'll cross paths with a tiny island fox or get buzzed by a dive-bombing peregrine falcon.

Island hikes range from simple beach walks to steep, loose, rocky rambles. The trail network consists mostly of retired ranch roads and narrow footpaths and is mostly (but not always) well marked, particularly at trailheads and junctions. You'll find a wide variety of hikes on the islands: easy nature walks, moderate hikes, and all-day adventures.

Looking for peace and solitude? You'll find it on the hike to Lester Point on San Miguel and on many other islands trails.

Island visitors can hike into history: follow in the footsteps of the native Chumash, discover a distinctive ranching history, and spot offshore shipwrecks. In addition to the usual sort of out-and-back hikes, one-way hikes are possible on Santa Cruz by making judicious use of the Island Packers boat schedule.

Nearly every hike leads to stunning overlooks, hidden beaches, and coves, and offers the opportunity to walk through a diversity of island habitats. You'll find yourself stopping often, soaking in the moment, and its surroundings. Hiking on the islands is always intriguing, even intoxicating at times.

When you head out on an island hike, be sure to bring along field glasses and a camera. You never know what you might see. Unless it's super-foggy, you're sure to sight inspiring "islandscapes"—that is to say, landscapes and seascapes unique in all the world. As for sighting wildlife, on island or just offshore, your chances are quite good, but do remember all creatures great and small are very much on their own schedule!

Hike smart, reconnect with nature, and have a wonderful time on the trail.

Hike On.

John McKinney & Chuck Graham

CHANNEL ISLANDS
NATIONAL PARK

Geography

It's theorized that the islands rose out of the Pacific through volcanic action some 14 million years ago, later sinking and rising many times as glaciation alternated with massive melting. Though never connected above sea level with the Santa Monica Mountains the islands are a continuation of the mainland mountains and are composed of similar marine formations.

The four northern islands were linked, until about 20,000 years ago, into a super-island called *Santaroasae*, only to part company during the final glacial melt into the wave-sculpted islands we see today.

During the Late Pleistocene, the islands were much closer to the mainland due to lower sea levels. Columbian mammoths swam from the mainland to Santarosae. As the Northern Chain evolved, isolation on the isles increased. The mammoths experienced island dwarfism eventually becoming pygmy mammoth, the remains of which have been found on Santa Cruz, Santa Rosa, and San Miguel islands.

The Channel Islands within the national park extend along the Southern California coast from Point Conception near Santa Barbara to San Pedro. The national park totals 249,354 acres, half of which are under the ocean, and includes the islands of San Miguel 9,325 acres; Santa Rosa 52,794 acres; Anacapa 699 acres; Santa Barbara 639 acres and Santa Cruz 60,645 acres (of which 76 percent is owned by the Nature Conservancy, 24 percent by the National Park Service).

Natural Attractions

The islands' mild Mediterranean climate and isolation from the mainland have benefited plants that either were altered through evolution on the

The rare island oak, or island live oak, exists only on the Channel Islands.

mainland or have perished altogether. What you see on the islands are glimpses of what Southern California might have been like many hundreds of years ago.

Channel Islands National Park is botanically rich to say the least. Due to its size and topography, Santa Cruz Island alone possesses a diverse assemblage of habitats promoting hundreds of plant species, of which 75 percent are natives.

Hikers can experience a wide range of environments: coastal dunes and bluffs, grasslands, island oak woodlands, coastal sage scrub, pine groves, hardwood groves, chaparral, and dense riparian corridors. Freshwater wetlands can be found on Santa Cruz and

A rare succulent indeed: the Santa Cruz Island live-forever.

Santa Rosa Islands. Unique caliche habitat is found on San Miguel Island.

With the combination of consistent rain and fog drip, spring wildflowers can be outstanding on the Channel Islands. Due to moisture by fog drip year-round across the chain, some wildflowers bloom at least twice in a year. For example, on Santa Cruz, island morning glory blooms all year long.

Three native terrestrial animals dwell on the archipelago: the island deer mouse, the island spotted skunk, and the island fox. The deer mouse thrives on all five islands and manages to survive in environments with little water. Spotted skunks are found on Santa Cruz Island and especially on Santa Rosa

The island scrub-jay lives only on Santa Cruz Island—meaning it has the smallest range of any North American bird species.

Island, where the population is estimated to be more than three thousand skunks.

If there was an iconic islands creature, surely it would be the island fox, found on Santa Cruz, Santa Rosa, and San Miguel islands. A good bit smaller than its mainland ancestor the gray fox, the island fox measures about a foot high and weighs in at 4 to 5 pounds.

Hikers will have a good chance of seeing an island fox. Other species of fox hunt only at night to avoid predators, but island foxes have no predators, so they're active during daylight hours. Not at all a picky eater, the island fox eats crabs, lizards, insects, fruits, birds, and lots of deer mice.

The iconic island fox, back from the edge of extinction and now thriving on Santa Cruz, Santa Rosa and San Miguel islands.

Birdlife on the Channel Islands—land birds, shorebirds and seabirds—is unique, diverse, and prolific. Nearly 400 species of birds have been tallied across the archipelago.

The Islands offer some of the best, last habitat for several once endangered and threatened species. Population recovery efforts and habitat restoration have been integral to the mission of Channel Islands National Park since its creation in 1980. Happily, this had led to notable conservation success stories.

After suffering from the aftereffects of DDT for decades and becoming extinct on the islands, bald eagles returned in 2002. Today, more than 50 bald eagles fly the skies over Channel Islands National Park. The same holds true for peregrine falcon, the world's fastest

A peregrine falcon, fastest bird in the world, zooms over Pelican Bay on Santa Cruz Island.

creature, which now thrives across the chain. After a 100-year absence due to egg collecting and other stressors, the common murre returned to its southerly haunts on Prince Island (off San Miguel) in 2011.

Fall and spring migrations are exciting times for birding the Channel Islands National Park. Due to their proximity to the Pacific Flyway, the islands serve as a haven for tired, bewildered, hungry birds migrating north and south. Gale force winds can blow birds off course, and the islands are a strategically placed rest stop for birds to recover and reboot before that innate tug calls them to continue. The list of oddities or rarities that touch down on the chain continues to grow, and includes summer tanager, ovenbird, sage thrasher, red-breasted nuthatch, black-throated blue warbler, bobolink, and mountain bluebirds.

If you're a visitor to the Channel Islands National Park, embrace its birdlife. You don't have to be a bird nerd to realize that these islands represent a diverse habitat welcoming to all species.

While en route to the Channel Islands, ferry passengers often observe marine life. Island Packers' captain and crew are always on the lookout for the many species of whales and dolphins that frequent the Santa Barbara Channel. The channel teems with cetaceans, and during various times of the year you may encounter blue and humpback whales, migrating gray whales and minke and fin whales. The apex predator of the channel are pods of transient orca that are encountered several times a year.

The most frequently seen dolphins are common dolphins, a great indicator of how healthy the channel is. Offshore bottlenose, Risso's, and Pacific white-sided dolphins are also seen in the channel.

Point Bennett on San Miguel Island possesses the largest congregation of seal and sea lions in the world. At any time of the year, there can be at least 30,000 pinnipeds breeding, pupping and hauled out on wind-groomed beaches and coves. Most of those animals are harbor seals, northern elephant seals, northern fur seals and California sea lions, but occasionally Guadalupe fur seals and stellar sea lions visit the rugged outpost.

Other islands have healthy populations of seals and sea lions, creatures that take advantage of the isolation and protected surrounding waters for their survival.

History

The remains of "Arlington Springs Man" are estimated to be just over 13,000 years old—possibly the oldest-known human remains in North America. Radiocarbon dating of fire areas on the island suggest humans may have inhabited the islands 30,000 years ago!

When Europeans first arrived in 1542, the northern Channel Islands were inhabited by an estimated two to three thousand Chumash, with a rich maritime culture and many villages on Santa Cruz and Santa Rosa islands, and a few on San Miguel as well.

The Chumash constructed the *tomol*, a versatile and sturdy plank canoe, considered the oldest example of ocean watercraft in North America. With their tomol, the Chumash paddled far and wide and developed a complex trade network amongst their communities on the various islands, and with native/nonnative communities on the mainland.

During the 19th century and well into the 20th, the islands were privately owned. Large sheep and cattle ranches spread out over Santa Cruz, Santa Rosa, and San Miguel islands.

Chumash paddle 23 miles from the mainland to Limuw (Santa Cruz Island) on their annual Tomol Channel Crossing.

On San Miguel, a monument to Juan Rodriguez Cabrillo, first European to set foot on what is now California and the Channel Islands.

In 1938, Santa Barbara and Anacapa islands were designated a national monument. Five of the eight Channel Islands—Anacapa, San Miguel, Santa Barbara, Santa Cruz, and Santa Rosa—became America's 40th national park in 1980. (The U.S. Navy owns San Nicholas and San Clemente islands. Farther south, famed Santa Catalina Island has pursued a destiny apart.) The waters surrounding the national park islands are protected as the Channel Islands National Marine Sanctuary.

Channel Islands Resources

Channel Islands National Marine Sanctuary protects 1,470 square miles of ocean waters around the Northern Channel Islands: Anacapa, Santa Cruz, Santa Rosa, San Miguel, and Santa Barbara islands. The sanctuary protects endangered species and sensitive habitats, and promotes research, education, and conservation projects in coordination with the National Oceanic and Atmospheric Research Administration. Learn more at channelislands.noaa.gov; 805-893-6416.

The Santa Cruz Island Foundation is a non-profit public benefit corporation established in 1985 by the late Carey Stanton "to collect, maintain, and catalog items of real and personal property or interests regarding Santa Cruz Island and the other California Channel Islands, unique island environments off the coast of Southern California." Learn more at scifoundation. org; 805-220-6414.

Author and Santa Cruz Island director Marla Daily is the creative force behind the comprehensive islapedia. com, an online California Islands encyclopedia.

Channel Islands Restoration is a non-profit that specializes in restoring habitat on the Channel Islands and adjacent mainland. It sponsors habitat restoration volunteer trips (i.e., ice plant removal on Anacapa island) on the islands with a focus on invasive plant management and propagating native plants. Learn more at cirweb.org; 805-448-5726.

Channel Islands Park Foundation's mission is to "Connect the community to Channel Islands

National Park to inspire stewardship through education, communications to current supporters and strategic outreach to underrepresented populations and millennials, and fun(d)raising."

Planning Your Trip

Advance planning for all hikes on the Channel Islands is highly recommended.

Keep in mind the islands are only publicly accessible by park concessionaire boats (Island Packers) and camping reservations are required for all of the park's campgrounds through recreation.gov

Services are very limited. No food is available, and water is extremely limited. Cell phone coverage is limited, as are emergency services should you become ill or injured.

Would-be adventurers enjoy the visitor center in Ventura Harbor as an exciting sneak preview of the splendid park out there in the open ocean, 12 to 60 miles away, a series of rugged, volcanic isles floating on the horizon. The visitor center boasts excellent island history and ecology exhibits and provides boat transportation information.

Robert J. Lagomarsino Visitor Center at Channel Islands National Park is located at 1901 Spinnaker Dr, Ventura, CA 93001. Phone: 805-658-5730. The visitor center is open every day, except

Thanksgiving and Christmas, from 8:30AM–5:00 PM. Channel Island National Park headquarters is located in the same complex as the visitor center. Phone: Business/Administration: 805-658-5700; Visitor Information at 1901 Spinnaker Dr., Ventura, CA 93001; 805-658-5730.

Most visitation occurs during the summer, but other seasons certainly have their attractions. Winter brings the opportunity to watch for migrating gray whales. Spectacular wildflower displays attract visitors in spring. Autumn certainly has its fans among hikers. The days are usually sunny, but not too hot, with minimal winds and clear ocean waters.

Frequent ferries deliver hikers and campers to Scorpion Anchorage on Santa Cruz, the most visited locale in the national park.

Scorpion Anchorage on Santa Cruz Island is the most visited area in the park for both hikers and campers. Anacapa Island is a particularly popular day trip.

The park's two small islands are compact enough that you can hike every trail on them in a day. The short boat trip to Anacapa takes you to two miles of trail. After the long voyage to remote Santa Barbara Island, you'll find five miles of trail to explore.

Campgrounds are available on each of the five islands allowing for a handful of hikes to be had on a single island camping trip. Campsites are available by reservation at recreation.gov. More possibilities abound by island hopping, bagging several diverse hikes while enjoying a memorable island experience via Island Packers.

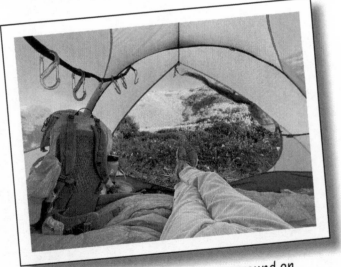

Room with a view in Scorpion Campground on Santa Cruz Island.

Boat Transportation

Island Packers has been transporting visitors to the Channel Islands since 1968. Located in the Ventura and Channel Islands Harbors, hikers can explore and plan all their island transportation at islandpackers.com or call 805-642-1393.

Island Packers offers options to island hop, offering visitors the opportunity to explore multiple islands on one excursion without going back and forth from the mainland.

Water is available on Santa Cruz and Santa Rosa Islands, but not the other islands. Hikers and campers will need to be self-sufficient, especially in the backcountry where the weather can turn at any time.

Leaping dolphins, spy-hopping whales, and rainbows. The voyage to the Channel Islands can be a magical, memorable adventure.

Look for giant coreopsis and gulls galore on the hike to Anacapa Island's picturesque lighthouse.

EVERY TRAIL TELLS A STORY.

I

ANACAPA ISLAND

HIKE ON.

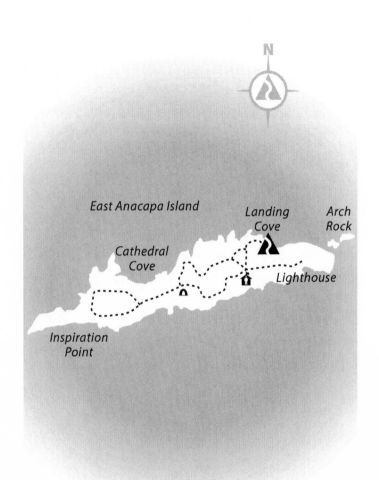

East Anacapa Island

Landing
Cove

Arch
Rock

Cathedral
Cove

Lighthouse

Inspiration
Point

TheTrailmaster.com

ANACAPA ISLAND

LOOP TRAIL

2 miles round trip

Anacapa, 12 miles southwest of Port Hueneme, is the Channel Island easiest to reach. It's a short (well, shorter voyage than to the other islands) ferry ride on an Island Packers boat. Anacapa offers the hiker a small sample size of the larger islands to the west.

Narrowest island in the national park, Anacapa is really three islets chained together with reefs that rise above the surface during low tide. Eastern and Middle Anacapa are mostly flat plateaus. Western Anacapa is hillier and boasts Anacapa's high point, 936-foot-high Summit Peak. The Chumash knew the isle as *Anyapakh*, translated as "ever changing," and likely refers to Anacapa's appearance from the mainland, which varies between one island and three.

The east isle, where the national park has a visitor center, is the light of the Channel Islands; a lighthouse and foghorn warn ships of the dangerous channel. It's a romantic approach to East Anacapa as you sail past Arch Rock. Below the tall wind-and-wave-cut cliffs, sea lions bark amongst the crashing breakers.

What you find on top depends on the time of year. In December and January, you may enjoy the sight of 30-ton gray whales passing south on their way to calving and mating waters off Baja California. In early spring, the giant coreopsis, one of the island's featured attractions, is something to behold. It is called the tree sunflower, an awkward thick-trunked perennial that grows as tall as 10 feet.

From April to June, visitors can observe (can't miss!) seeing, hearing, and smelling thousands of Western gulls busy nesting on the island. Free from the mainland predators, such as foxes, coyotes and eagles, the gulls here are quite loud and territorial. Some hikers like a spring adventure traipsing past the birds; some do not.

Other commonly sighted birds on East Anacapa include peregrine falcon, Brandt's cormorant, Allen's hummingbird, rufous-crowned sparrow, and orange-crowned warbler. West Anacapa hosts one of the state's largest colonies of California brown pelicans.

The visitor center offers history and nature displays and a look at the old light from the historic lighthouse. From the visitor center, you can hike a figure-eight loop and see all the sights. The short trail to the lighthouse is an easy add-on.

DIRECTIONS: Island Packers offers frequent trips to Anacapa. The boat lands at a dock (the only access to the isle), and from here you ascend 150 stairs or so to the top of the cliffs near the island's visitor center.

THE HIKE: Head out along the north shore of the isle and soon reach Cathedral Cove, where there's an overlook that offers views of a rocky shore frequented by sea lions and harbor seals. The path swings inland to the island's seven-site campground, then splits.

Hike west toward Inspiration Point; the southern loop passes a Chumash midden site and past stands of giant coreopsis, glorious in Spring bloom, lifeless when dormant. At Inspiration Point, look westward over Middle Anacapa, with Santa Cruz Island looming large in the background.

Return to the campground and this time continue along the southern branch of the trail to Pinniped Point, where you can gaze down at the pinnipeds—sea lions and harbors seals—that often haul out on the rocky beach.

Finish your island tour with a short hike to just shy of the lighthouse, which dates from 1932 and was automated in 1966. With the lighthouse's once-a-minute beeping ringing in your ears, head back to where you began your island circle tour.

Seaside daisies line the awesome coastal trail leading to Cavern Point.

EVERY TRAIL TELLS A STORY.

II
SANTA CRUZ ISLAND

HIKE ON.

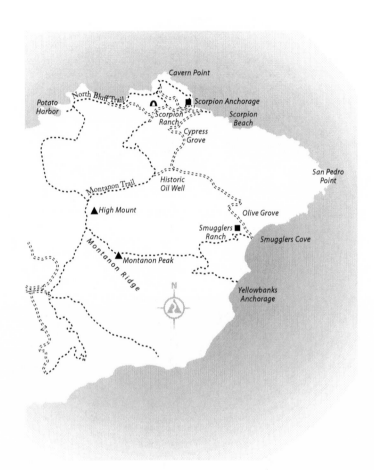

Cavern Point

North Bluff Trail

Potato
Harbor

Scorpion Anchorage

Scorpion
Ranch

Scorpion
Beach

Cypress
Grove

San Pedro
Point

Montanon Trail

Historic
Oil Well

▲ High Mount

Olive Grove

Smugglers
Ranch ■

Smugglers Cove

Montanon Ridge

▲ Montanon Peak

Yellowbanks
Anchorage

N

Cavern Point & Potato Harbor

Cavern Point Loop Trail, North Bluff Trail

From Scorpion Anchorage to Cavern Point is 2 miles round trip with 300-foot elevation gain; to Potato Harbor is 5 miles round trip

Santa Cruz offers hikers plenty of room to roam, as well as a far-reaching trail system composed mainly of old ranch roads. The only limitation on the hiker seems to be time: day-trippers are allowed about five hours on the island before it's necessary to catch the boat back to Ventura Harbor.

For first timers to the isle, we recommend the hike from Scorpion Anchorage to Cavern Point and then on to Potato Harbor. It's a great intro to the isle and serves as a kind of scouting expedition for future visits and possibly more challenging hikes.

A short walk from the Scorpion Anchorage leads to picnic tables, restrooms and a historic two-story ranch house. In the 1880s, a colony of French and Italian immigrants led by Justinian Caire began a Mediterranean-style ranch here, raising sheep and cattle, growing olives and almonds, and even making wine. The Gherini family, descendants of Caire, owned the east end of the isle until 1997, when the property was added to the national park.

The old ranch bunkhouse, transformed into a modest visitor center, offers displays about the island's natural attractions and colorful history.

The short, but steep, climb on Cavern Point Trail leads the hiker to a stunning viewpoint. Look for seals and sea lions bobbing in the waters around the point, as well as cormorants, pigeon guillemots and black oystercatchers swooping along the rugged volcanic cliffs. You're likely to see ravens, California brown pelicans and peregrine falcons as well.

From here, you can hike along the cliffs to Potato Harbor, surely one of the loveliest anchorages on the island. The postcard-perfect harbor is framed by white rocks, a 112-foot-high rock pinnacle and a small arch. Depending on the winds and tides, Potato Harbor can be a welcome place for sailors to drop anchor or a tricky, even down-right dangerous place to maneuver in and out of.

DIRECTIONS: Just west of the dock near the visitor center, join the signed footpath leading north.

THE HIKE: The first part of the trail (about 0.3 mile) is a very steep ascent. Reward for the climb is an awesome clear-day view of the coast from Ventura all the way up to Point Conception. And the views inland over the island are pretty good, too!

Continue westward on the clifftop trail to Cavern Point, which sits atop a trio of sea caves known as Neptune's Trident. From Cavern Point, you can choose to close the loop (to complete a 2-mile hike) by descending the western leg of the loop trail (a dirt road) to Scorpion Ranch. The loop trail descends into the back end of the lower campground.

Otherwise follow the clifftop trail a mile to a junction with Potato Harbor Road (possible return route), then continue to Potato Harbor Overlook. Enjoy the views of Potato Harbor, the mainland, and the wide blue Pacific.

Return the same way or take an optional return route: retrace your steps 0.7 mile to a junction and join right-forking Potato Harbor Road. After a mellow start, the road drops steeply into Scorpion Canyon near the upper campground. Follow Scorpion Canyon Loop Trail to return to the visitor center and the trailhead where you began this hike.

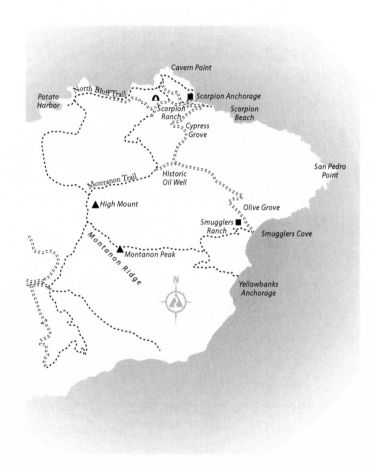

Cavern Point

North Bluff Trail

Potato Harbor

Scorpion Anchorage ■

Scorpion Ranch

Scorpion Beach

Cypress Grove

San Pedro Point

Montanon Trail

Historic Oil Well

▲ *High Mount*

Olive Grove

Smugglers Ranch ■

Smugglers Cove

Montanon Ridge

▲ *Montanon Peak*

N

Yellowbanks Anchorage

Scorpion Canyon Loop

Smugglers Road, Scorpion Canyon Trails

4.5 miles round trip with 700-foot elevation gain

The hike in-and-out of Scorpion Canyon is an excellent, semi-tough intro to the charms of Santa Cruz Island. Attractions include stellar vistas over the isle, a side trip to a curious oil well, and an opportunity to take a peek at the island scrub jay, said to be the only island-endemic species of bird in all of North America.

First things first, and fair warning. Yes, it's a loop trail and you can hike it from either direction. That said, you want to hike this trail clockwise, so you accomplish the elevation gain first and then drop into Scorpion Canyon. It's a thigh-burning exercise just descending into the canyon, much less climbing out of it.

A word about the island scrub jay, a slightly larger, brighter blue version of the mainland species. While mainlander scrub jays are found everywhere in SoCal from the backcountry to backyards, the island scrub jay has the distinction of being the bird species with the smallest range on the North American continent.

DIRECTIONS: From the pier at Scorpion, head up the trail about 0.1 mile and look left for the signed trail.

THE HIKE: Join Smugglers Road and ascend south. The road soon delivers vistas of the beach, beachgoers, kayakers and, about a half mile along, Anacapa Island. Look for a short trail leading to a small grove of Monterey cypress. "Delphine's Grove" was planted in the late 1800s by Delphine Caire, daughter of island owner Justinian Caire. (A May 2020 wildfire burned through the grove; many of the trees collapsed after getting scorched. At this writing, the grove is off limits.)

About 1.7 miles out, reach a junction and bear right toward Scorpion Canyon Loop. Your route gentles for a bit then reaches the hike's highest point near the oil well and junction with Scorpion Canyon Trail.

Walk over to check out the oil well, constructed by Atlantic Richfield Company (ARCO) in 1966. Drilling reached a thousand feet down—and water not oil. Apparently not discouraged, Scorpion Ranch owners leased the well to Union Oil but…the infamous Santa Barbara Oil Spill occurred in 1969 from a blown Union Oil rig. To say the least, public sentiment turned against further oil exploration in the channel. Take a moment to be thankful this artifact is the only reminder of oil drilling on the islands and Santa Cruz Island doesn't resemble, say, Huntington Beach with its rows of ceaselessly drilling wells.

Bear right to join Scorpion Canyon Trail and begin a super-steep descent. Slow and easy now and watch your footing on the rocky slopes. At first the trail follows the old oil pipeline down the ridgeline, and you can spot remnants of the pipe.

Enjoy vistas of the mountainous interior of the island and across to lovely Santa Barbara on the mainland. When you reach an oak woodland, keep an eye out for the island scrub jay.

At the three-mile mark, you hit bottom and follow a path through a smaller canyon to the campground, then back to the beach and landing.

The hike through rugged Scorpion Canyon offers a semi-tough intro to Santa Cruz Island.

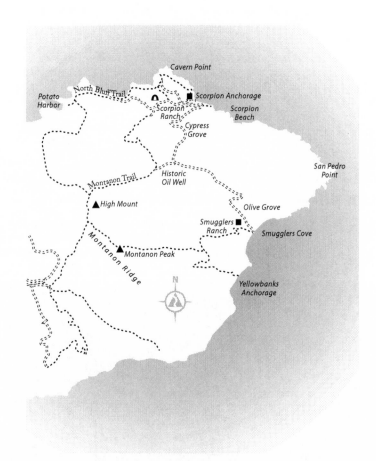

Cavern Point

North Bluff Trail

Potato
Harbor

Scorpion Anchorage

Scorpion
Ranch

Scorpion
Beach

Cypress
Grove

San Pedro
Point

Montanon Trail

Historic
Oil Well

▲ High Mount

Montanon Ridge

Olive Grove

Smugglers
Ranch

Smugglers Cove

▲ Montanon Peak

N

Yellowbanks
Anchorage

MONTAÑON RIDGE

MONTAÑON, SMUGGLERS CANYON TRAILS

**Loop from Scorpion Anchorage over Montañon Ridge is
10 miles round trip with 1,800-foot elevation gain**

Montañon Peak (1,808 feet) is the highest summit in the national park accessible to hikers. Mount
Diablo (Picacho del Diablo, elevation 2,450 feet)
ranks as the highest peak on Santa Cruz; however,
it—and other high points along North Ridge—are
in The Nature Conservancy area of the isle and thus
off-limits to hikers.

When viewed from Ventura or Santa Barbara
shores, Santa Cruz Island doesn't look *that* big. However, hike a trail up to the commanding Montañon
Ridge promontories, and the island appears massive:
row upon row of mountains alternating with deep
canyons, as well as a seemingly endless series of stark
bluffs extending to the horizon.

Skilled hikers with navigation skills have been
making a circle loop popularly known as Montañon

Ridge Loop Trail for years; however, closing the circle after reaching Montañon Ridge meant rock scrambling and navigating a sketchy trail. This was once an old sheep trail during the island's ranching era. After the sheep were removed in 1998, the path served for 20 years as a "social trail" for hikers. In 2018, the trail got a major rehab and was added to the official NPS trail system.

The Montañon Ridge Loop is arguably the prettiest and most rugged hike on Santa Cruz Island. Because of its length and difficulty, the trail would be a challenge for most hikers to complete during the time allotted on an Island Packers day trip. In most cases this is a hike better left to campers, who have a full day to roam.

DIRECTIONS: You'll begin this hike by walking to the campground.

THE HIKE: From the pier at Scorpion Anchorage walk past the bathrooms, old ranching implements and Cavern Point Trailhead on the right. Continue along the dirt road to the upper campground in Scorpion Canyon. The sign for Montañon Ridge Loop Trail is located just before reaching Potato Harbor.

The trail leads a short distance southeast, then bends southwest and ascends several marine terraces above steep, open book-shaped canyons. The trail rises above dreamy Potato Harbor, wave battered

Coche Point and massive Chinese Harbor. Enjoy stupendous vistas of the north side of the island while walking amongst California fuchsia, bladderpod, and Santa Cruz Island liveforever. You might hear barking and bellowing wafting up to your location from two California sea lion rookeries located below the sheer, volcanic cliffs between Potato Harbor and Coche Point.

The trail veers southeast and rolls upward away from Chinese Harbor. Shortly thereafter, the narrow track bends southwest and makes a steep, quick ascent to a narrow, rocky ridge (that will eventually connect with the Montañon Ridge Trail). Follow the ridge east between dense clusters of island buckwheat

Challenging Montañon Ridge Trail literally and figuratively hits the highpoints of the island.

towards a steep, rocky spire. The trail then veers just beneath the exposed summit on the northside, traveling amidst a canopy of island oak trees.

During spring, this is a great place to see wildflowers: fragrant lupine, giant coreopsis, and the low-growing Santa Cruz Island silver lotus. Continue your hike along the rocky, rolling spine, decorated with multicolored lichen, toward Montañon Ridge Trail.

Montañon Ridge Loop Trail converges with Montañon Ridge Trail. From this junction, it's about 1.5 miles to Montañon Peak. To reach the peak, follow the narrow, rolling spine southeast on Montañon Ridge Trail.

To return to Scorpion Anchorage, the route veers northeast and descends the rocky ridge to an open saddle.

From the junction where Montañon Ridge Loop Trail and Montañon Ridge Trail converge, descend northeast to the exposed saddle. On days when northwest winds are especially stiff, hikers will be exposed to those howling winds across this saddle choked in island buckwheat. Sweeping island vistas will also expand with the Anacapa Passage and Anacapa Island on the immediate eastern horizon. On extremely clear days look for Santa Barbara, Santa Catalina, and San Nicholas islands, three of the four isles.

From the old oil drill site, hikers can return by way of a very steep and rocky descent into Scorpion Canyon and continue to the upper and lower campgrounds then back to Scorpion Anchorage.

An easier return route is to head right (southeast) on the road to Smugglers Cove. You'll follow the road back to a last overlook and another stupendous view: Scorpion Rock, the southeast fringe of Santa Cruz Island, and Anacapa Island.

Wind-sculpted island oaks cling to life on the rocky spine of the island.

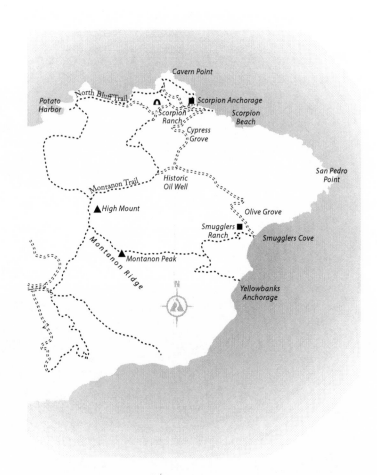

Cavern Point

North Bluff Trail

Potato Harbor

Scorpion Anchorage

Scorpion Ranch

Scorpion Beach

Cypress Grove

San Pedro Point

Montanon Trail

Historic Oil Well

▲ High Mount

Olive Grove

Smugglers Ranch ■

Smugglers Cove

Montanon Ridge

▲ Montanon Peak

Yellowbanks Anchorage

N

TheTrailmaster.com

SMUGGLERS COVE

SMUGGLERS ROAD TRAIL

**From Scorpion Anchorage to Smugglers Cove is 7.4 miles
round trip with 800-foot elevation gain**

As the story goes, Smugglers Cove, with its iso-
lated location (yet close to the mainland), hosted an
assortment of smugglers from Spanish contraband-
istas to Prohibition-era bootleggers. While by no
means a secret beach today, Smugglers Cove is lightly
visited and the trail to it lightly traveled. By any
standard this is a standout shoreline, one of the great
beauties of coastal California.

Don't expect many amenities, but Smugglers
Cove does offer a couple of picnic benches and a pit
toilet. A sign there welcomes you to Channel Islands
National Park, though likely it was posted to welcome boaters, not hikers.

If you're on an island day trip, calculate the time
needed to trek to Smugglers Cove and back. Figure 4
to 5 hours so don't attempt this hike unless you have

sufficient time and/or happen to be a fast hiker. One challenge is the uphill hiking—coming AND going—first the ascent from Scorpion Anchorage, then the climb from Smugglers Cove on the way back. Having said that, it's also true a goodly portion of the hike is on flat, well graded road.

Fans of the curious succulents will find a wide variety of dudleya dotting rocky terrain en route. Also be on the lookout for piles of white stones, traces of the original (1892) road constructed to connect Scorpion Anchorage to Smugglers Cove.

DIRECTIONS: From the pier at Scorpion, head up the trail about 0.1 mile and look left for the trail sign.

THE HIKE: Join Smugglers Road (which you'll follow all the way to the cove) and ascend south. The road soon delivers vistas of the beach, beachgoers and kayakers, and about a half mile along, a view of Anacapa Island. Look for a short trail leading to a small grove of Monterey cypress. "Delphine's Grove" was planted in the late 1800s by Delphine Caire, daughter of island owner Justinian Caire. (A May 2020 wildfire burned through the grove; many of the trees collapsed after getting scorched. At this writing, the grove is off limits.)

Reach a junction at about the 1.7-mile mark; the right fork leads to a meet-up with Montañon Ridge Trail and Scorpion Canyon Loop. Stay left and, after a bit less than a mile's travel, descend steeply. When you pass olive groves on either side of the road, you might imagine you're hiking on a Greek island. Considering that the trees have been neglected for so long, they look pretty good. Santa Cruz Island Olive Oil, anyone?

As you near shore, you'll be hit by a pleasant sea breeze and inhale the tang of salt air. Walk the splendid beach, brave the cold water and take a swim. And remember to hike back in time to catch your boat back to the mainland.

Onward to Smugglers Cove, a standout shoreline by any standard.

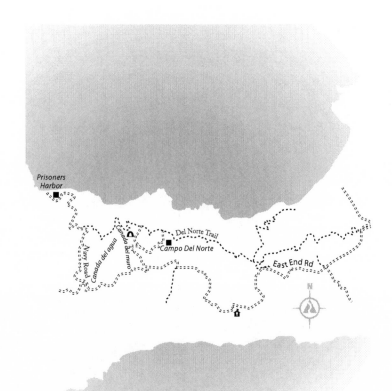

PELICAN BAY

PELICAN TRAIL

From Prisoners Harbor to Pelican Bay is 5 miles round trip with 800-foot elevation gain.

Here's your one chance to hike beyond national park boundaries on the only trail open to the public on The Nature Conservancy property on Santa Cruz Island. The trail offers a sampling of the island's steep gullies and rocky canyons, as well as its abundant native flora. But wait, there's more: stunning views of Prisoners Harbor east to Chinese Harbor and Coche Point and, as you follow the trail northwest, dreamy vistas of Pelican Bay and Tinkers Cove.

Passengers on the Island Packers boat are required sign an acknowledgement of risk waiver before hiking Pelican Trail. That waver can be signed at the Island Packers office or on the way out on the ferry. After disembarking the Island Packers boat, day trippers will listen to an island orientation delivered by a crewmember or a volunteer naturalist.

Afterwards, those wanting to hike out to Pelican Bay can do so on their own. Access to The Nature Conservancy trail is also permitted to private boaters with a valid landing permit. Visit nature.org/cruzpermit

From 1910 to 1937 Ira and Margaret Eaton's "Pelican Bay Camp" advertised itself as a sportsman's paradise for wild boar hunting and sword fishing. The three-hour voyage from Santa Barbara cost $10 with "excellent meals and comfortable cabins" an additional $5 a day.

Silent-era moviemakers were attracted to remote and photogenic Pelican Bay. Hikers will find that same natural beauty along Pelican Trail, as well as an abundance of native flora: island hazardia (aka island bristleweed), island buckwheat, giant coreopsis, manzanita, island morning glory, and more. Keep an eye out for island foxes, as well as bald eagles flying by.

DIRECTIONS: From the shaded picnic area at Prisoners Harbor, walk the dirt road past the historic corral and two brick warehouses. Take the first dirt road on the right that leads to a locked gate. This is the property line for The Nature Conservancy. Just before that, also on the right is the trailhead for Pelican Trail.

THE HIKE: From the trailhead, the initial path is steep and rocky, leading to an old lookout post left over from the ranching area. Ranching spanned from the 1820s; the last of the ranch animals were removed in 2008. The lookout is now an interpretive site.

From the lookout, the narrow trail meanders through dense oak woodland habitat and winds its way toward the ocean. Magnificent views open to the east before the trail curves back to the northwest. You'll have a good chance of spotting an island scrub jay, a rare bird indeed, with the smallest range of any avian species in North America.

Continuing northwesterly toward Pelican Bay, the trail leads through oak groves and past ironwood trees and Bishop Pines (Santa Cruz Island is the southernmost part of the pine's range).

Just before reaching Pelican Bay, consider stopping for lunch at Tinkers Cove, a secluded, cobbled beach. The cove is named after Tinker Bell; scenes from the first Peter Pan movie were filmed here in 1924.

From Tinkers Cove, it's a quick rock-hop west up the drainage to the overlook at Pelican Bay, a favorite anchorage for private boaters.

Pelican Trail leads to lupine-framed lookout above Prisoners Harbor.

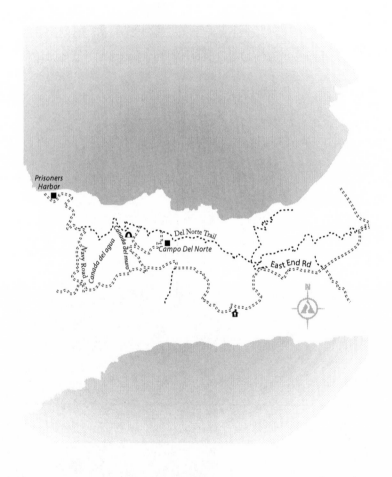

Prisoners
Harbor

Del Norte Trail

Campo Del Norte

Cañada del muro

Cañada del agua

Navy Road

East End Rd

N

DEL NORTE

OLD NAVY ROAD, DEL NORTE TRAILS

From Prisoners Harbor to Del Norte Campground is 7 miles round trip with 700-foot elevation gain

The island's only backcountry campsite is located at Del Norte, accessible by a moderately strenuous hike from Prisoners Harbor. The route weaves through a series of canyons and oak woodlands, as well as over ridges, before reaching the campground.

Best way to go is via Old Navy Road and Del Norte Trail. You could opt to stay on Old Navy Road for the trek to the campground, which does offer fine vistas of the isle's south side, but it's a longer (10 miles round trip) and more challenging (1,200-foot gain) way to go.

You'll begin the hike from the pier at idyllic Prisoners Harbor, which lies right on the boundary between lands owned by Channel Islands National Park (CINP) and The Nature Conservancy (TNC).

BTW, CINP owns 24 percent, the southeast part of the island, and TNC owns the other 76 percent.

No water is available at the campground, so bring plenty for day hiking, and plenty more if you're backpacking. The camp offers four scenic campsites amidst an oak grove and good views over the north side of the island.

You have a good chance to sight an island scrub jay in Del Norte's environs. The island scrub jay has the smallest range of any bird in North America, is a third size larger and possesses a deeper blue than its mainland cousin—the Western scrub jay. An estimated 2,000 of them thrive on Santa Cruz Island. Birders travel from all over to see this flash of blue in the island's oak groves. Each adult jay caches between 3,500 to 6,000 (!) acorns per year, and are also known as "eco engineers of the island."

DIRECTIONS: After a 90-minute boat ride on Island Packers, day hikers will disembark onto the pier, and then listen to an island orientation given by a crew member or a volunteer naturalist. "Fox boxes" are available at Prisoners Harbor to store any gear visitors want to leave behind before hiking to Del Norte.

THE HIKE: Leave the shaded area just south of the pier and walk the road past the corral and the two historic, brick warehouses used during the island's ranching era. Note the restored freshwater estuary on the left—an excellent birdwatching spot. Continue south, past a dirt road on the right, across a seasonal creek bed and another dirt road on the right. Continue with Old Navy Road as it bends eastward, steepening quickly with terrific vistas of Prisoners Harbor.

You'll intersect Del Norte Trail 1.5 miles from the pier. Leave the gravel road and follow the narrow trail east. Before the trail bends southeast, you'll spot a picnic table situated with a nice view of Chinese Harbor and Coche Point. The trail winds up and down through two riparian corridors—Cañada del Agua and Cañada del Muro—to a junction with Del Norte Road. Follow the road 0.2 mile to the campground.

The pier at Prisoners Harbor is the trailhead for terrific hikes exploring this side of the island.

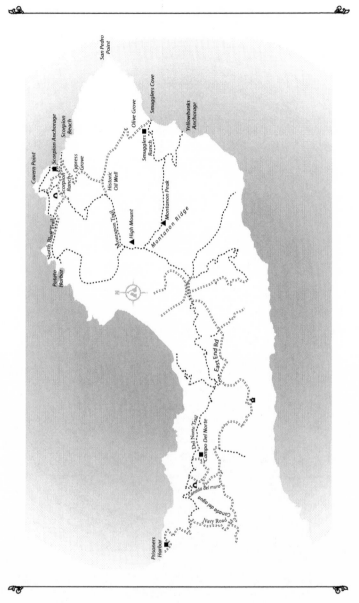

San Pedro Point

Smugglers Cove

Olive Grove

Yellowbanks Anchorage

Scorpion Anchorage
Scorpion Beach

Smugglers Ranch

Cavern Point

Scorpion Ranch
Cypress Grove

Historic Oil Well

Montanon Peak

Montanon Trail

High Mount

Montanon Ridge

North Bluff Trail

Potato Harbor

East End Rd

Del Norte Trail
Campo Del Norte

Cañada del muro
Cañada de dos

Navy Road

Prisoners Harbor

TheTrailmaster.com

PRISONERS HARBOR TO SCORPION ANCHORAGE

OLD NAVY ROAD, DEL NORTE, MONTAÑON RIDGE TRAILS

14 miles one way with 1,300-foot elevation gain

Perhaps the most challenging hike on Santa Cruz Island, this grand tour leads eastward along a mountainous spine from Prisoners Harbor to Scorpion Anchorage, from a well vegetated environment to the more arid region on the isle's southeast end.

Bring plenty of water as there is no water source along the entire route until reaching the campgrounds in Scorpion Canyon. Some hikers may elect to do this in reverse from Scorpion Anchorage to Prisoners but be warned there is no water source at Prisoners Harbor.

Should you wish to camp at Scorpion Canyon after finishing this hike in a day, make sure your camping gear and food gets dropped off at the pier at Scorpion Anchorage before continuing on the Island Packers ferry to Prisoners Harbor.

DIRECTIONS: After disembarking the Island Packers ferry onto the pier at Prisoners Harbor, day trippers will listen to an island orientation delivered by an Island Packers crewmember or a volunteer naturalist. Begin on the Navy Road and walk past the old corral and brick warehouses on the right and the restored freshwater estuary on the left.

THE HIKE: Follow Navy Road for 1.5 miles to the Del Norte Trail junction. Head left and east on the steep, rolling single track trail to Del Norte Campground, 3.5 miles from the start. Continue straight and east with a steep ascent reconnecting with Navy Road. At this point, hikers are on the narrowest portion of the island, easily seeing both coastlines north and south.

Continue past a junction with the trail that heads left and northeast to Chinese Harbor. Keep hiking east to another trail junction. Left and north places hikers on China Pines Road. Just before that and bearing right and south takes hikers on the Loma Pelona Loop Road. Instead, continue east with Montañon Ridge dominating the eastern horizon. The trail fades a little here but remain on the narrow spine east to the ridgetop. Quite arid, the spine is cloaked in multi-colored lichen and island flora such as island buckwheat, Santa Cruz Island liveforever and prickly pear cactus.

As you ascend, it'll become obvious you're traveling in the correct direction, as both sides of the rocky spine steepen, and the trail is more defined. Once at the Montañon Ridge, a trail sign points northeastward and it's 4 miles to Scorpion Anchorage. Take a few moments and enjoy the island vistas from this lofty ridgetop along the Montañon Ridge Trail. On clear days most of the northside of the isle is visible. The summit of Montañon at 1,808 feet isn't far to the southeast, and the Anacapa Passage shimmers in the late afternoon sun.

Expect lots of loose rock on the descent—some hikers say it's like having ball bearings beneath your boots. However, once on the Montañon Ridge Trail, the route is straightforward all the way to the old oil well.

Once you reach the oil well, you have two options. Hikers can descend steep and rocky Scorpion Canyon on a trail that runs past the seasonal creek, the campgrounds and eventually to the pier at Scorpion Anchorage. Or continue 0.25 mile east to a road that leads to Smugglers Cove. If you go right and southeast it takes you to Smugglers Cover; instead, head left and north back to Scorpion Anchorage.

The more technical descent is the Scorpion Loop Trail, dropping sharply into the seasonal creek, past the upper and lower campgrounds, and eventually emptying out at the beach of Scorpion Anchorage.

Congratulations on completing a very hard hike! At the end of the hike, consider celebrating with a dive into the cool, clear waters of Scorpion Anchorage.

Santa Rosa Island at its most sublime: Lobo Canyon ranks with the top hikes in all of Southern California.

EVERY TRAIL TELLS A STORY.

III
SANTA ROSA
ISLAND

HIKE ON.

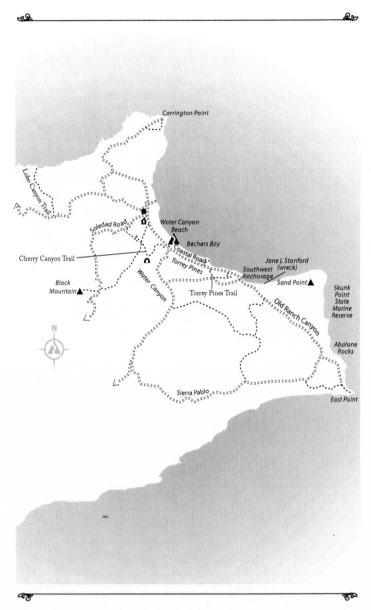

Carrington Point

Lobo Canyon Trail

Soledad Road

Water Canyon Beach

Bechers Bay

Cherry Canyon Trail

Coastal Road

Torrey Pines

Black Mountain ▲

Water Canyon

Torrey Pines Trail

Jane L Stanford (wreck)

Southwest Anchorage

Sand Point ▲

Skunk Point State Marine Reserve

Old Ranch Canyon

Abalone Rocks

N

Sierra Pablo

East Point

TheTrailmaster.com

CHERRY CANYON

CHERRY CANYON TRAIL

Loop through Cherry Canyon is 3.5 miles round trip with 300-foot elevation gain

Chock-full of native flora and offering great coastal views, the hike to and through Cherry Canyon offers an excellent intro to the isle for the time-short visitor.

A seasonal creek flows through Cherry Canyon, which abounds with flowering plants in spring: lupine, island poppy, Indian paintbrush, giant coreopsis, island liveforever, manzanita, monkey flower and more. Fog drip, not rain is the largest water input here; even during winters of little rain, there will likely be wildflowers blooming in Cherry Canyon in the spring and summer.

Birdsongs from the resident warblers and house finches add a musical accompaniment to your hike. Keep an eye out for the island fox, commonly sighted in these parts. And enjoy views from the top of the canyon—to the sweep of Bechers Bay and the Torrey pines forest, and to the oak-dotted hills of the island interior.

Note this hike can also be done in reverse. A stroll along Water Canyon Beach makes an ideal add-on to this short adventure Those familiar with crowded SoCal beaches will appreciate walking this little-visited, wide, white, windswept sand beach.

DIRECTIONS: From the pier, walk past the historic buildings and restrooms.

THE HIKE: From the pier, stroll through the historic Vail and Vickers Cattle Ranch. Veer southeast, keeping the old barn and corrals on the right. Walter L. Vail and J.V. Vickers began cattle ranching operations in the 1860s, and their families continued ranching Santa Rosa Island up until 1998.

After leaving the ranch site, head southeast on Coastal Road (keeping the dirt airstrip and the eroding coastal bluffs on your left). Near the entrance to Water Canyon Campground, veer right and west, and ascend a narrow, rocky track that offers a nice view of the 15 campsites in the campground. (Drinking water is available here.)

The trail hovers above the north side of Water Canyon, then veers north across a broad and flat marine terrace. Partake of tremendous vistas of the ranch site, the entirety of Bechers Bay, the long sandy finger of Skunk Point, the Santa Cruz Passage, and the rugged, mountainous northwest end of Santa Cruz Island.

Continue north a short distance past a junction with Telephone Road, which leads up to Black Mountain (elevation 1,298 feet, one of the island's highest summits). Anywhere on the marine terrace makes for a good lunch spot while soaking in mesmerizing island vistas. Afterward, the trail bends south and descends past a weathered but sturdy island oak embedded in the bluff. The trail then bears abruptly to the right and north.

As the trail gradually descends through Cherry Canyon, it eventually loops northeast and empties out onto Soledad Road. Follow the dirt road back to the ranch site, Bechers Bay, and the pier where the Island Packers ferry awaits.

Wildflowers abound in Cherry Canyon, including the island poppy, endemic to the Channel Islands.

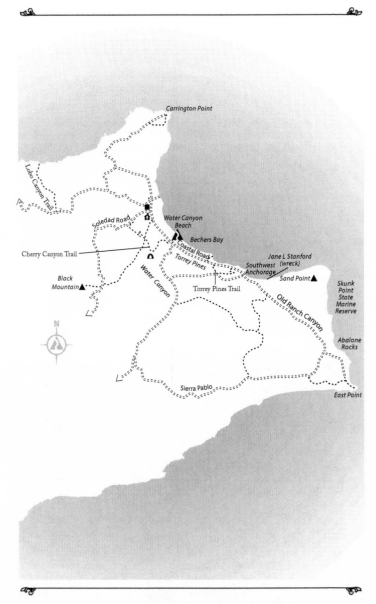

Carrington Point

Lobo Canyon Trail

Soledad Road

Water Canyon Beach

Cherry Canyon Trail

Bechers Bay

Coastal Road

Torrey Pines

Jane L Stanford (wreck)

Southwest Anchorage

Sand Point

Skunk Point State Marine Reserve

Black Mountain

Water Canyon

Torrey Pines Trail

Old Ranch Canyon

Abalone Rocks

N

Sierra Pablo

East Point

TORREY PINES

COASTAL ROAD, TORREY PINES TRAILS

From Pier to Torrey Pines with loop through grove is 5.6 miles round trip with 500-foot elevation gain.

A visit to the rare Torrey pines makes a marvelous day hike. One of the rarest pine species in North America, the Torrey pine grows only on Santa Rosa Island and 175 miles away across the Pacific on the mainland coast north of San Diego between Del Mar and La Jolla in Torrey Pines State Natural Reserve.

From the pier (or Water Canyon Campground if you happen to be staying there), you'll join Coastal Road that, true to its name, parallels the rugged shoreline, and leads you to upper and lower lengths of Torrey Pines Trail.

Wander the yellow dirt trail through the grove and gaze out at the individual trees, no two alike. From a distance, the pines appear tall, thick, unperturbable. Closer views reveal their trunks twisted and gnarled by years and years of strong winds. Branches, bowed, even broken, hold on, sometimes linking arms so to speak with other trees as if to keep from falling.

Visiting Santa Rosa's Torrey pines is a quite different experience from walking the trails in Torrey Pines State Natural Reserve. The island's Torrey pines attract a miniscule number of visitors compared to the San Diego County population, which attracts scores of locals and tourists from around the world.

The pines in Torrey Pines State Reserve look—and are—quite drought-stressed and it's easy to speculate the trees are suffering the effects of climate change with too little rainfall and too few foggy days. In contrast, botanists adjudge the island Torrey pines population to be healthy and stable.

The Torrey pines on Santa Rosa Island feature a dense cover of needles and branches, with pinecones scattered everywhere. There are places in the grove where branches block out the sun!

If you like the sound of wind lashing pines, you'll love taking this hike on a breezy day. The experience of lingering in the grove to escape the wind is one you'll long remember.

DIRECTIONS: Begin this hike on Coastal Road, easily accessible from the pier or landing strip.

THE HIKE: From the pier at Bechers Bay, walk past the historic Vail and Vickers Ranch heading southeast, then east, eventually joining Coastal Road as it bends parallel to the air strip Water Canyon Beach and the curve of Bechers Bay.

Continue past the entry to the campground on the right before descending a steep draw into Water Canyon. Cross the narrow footbridge and make a quick, steep ascent on Coastal Road. The road plateaus on a level marine terrace. The Torrey pines are in plain view!

The upper length of Torrey Pines Trail ascends above the stands of Torrey pines and offers grand views over the eastern part of Santa Rosa Island. The lower part of the loop trail leads along the bluffs and delivers fine coastal vistas.

Descend Torrey Pines Trail to Coastal Road, turn left, and return the way you came.

Hikers get great views of the rare Torrey pines. So do stand-up paddlers!

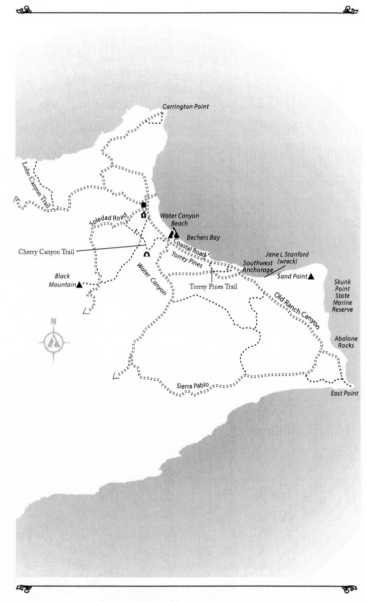

Carrington Point

Lobo Canyon Trail

Soledad Road

Water Canyon Beach

Bechers Bay

Cherry Canyon Trail

Coastal Road

Torrey Pines

Jane L Stanford (wreck)

Southwest Anchorage

Sand Point ▲

Skunk Point State Marine Reserve

Black Mountain ▲

Water Canyon

Torrey Pines Trail

Old Ranch Canyon

Abalone Rocks

N

Sierra Pablo

East Point

TheTrailmaster.com

BLACK MOUNTAIN

COASTAL ROAD, CHERRY CANYON, BLACK MOUNTAIN TRAILS

From Pier to Black Mountain is 8 miles round trip with 1,300-foot elevation gain

Beginning with Black Mountain (1,298 feet) this hike hits the high points on Santa Rosa Island. Reward for the strenuous ascent are fabulous island vistas—San Miguel Island to the northwest and Santa Cruz Island to the east/southeast. On ultra-clear days, the Santa Ynez Mountains, rising behind greater Santa Barbara, are visible on the mainland.

As the story goes, Black Mountain (aka Cerro Negro and Monte Negro) is named for the rather dark-leaved Island oak, found in several groves high in canyons on the mountain's shoulders.

You can extend this high-country hike with ascents of the two tallest summits on the island—Soledad Peak (1,574 feet) and Radar Mountain (1,589 feet). Plan on a full day of hiking!

This route can be transformed into a loop hike at the junction of where the Black Mountain Trail and Soledad Road converge at about 1,092 feet. To loop back, stay on Soledad Road heading northeast, and descending back to the ranch site and the pier.

DIRECTIONS: After disembarking the Island Packers ferry, visitors will listen to an island orientation, or a camper orientation delivered by the Santa Rosa Island ranger or volunteer naturalist. After leaving the pier, walk past the historic Vail and Vickers cattle ranch site, keeping the barn and corrals on the right. (If you're camped at the Water Canyon Campground, the hike will begin via the same route to Cherry Canyon.)

THE HIKE: From Coastal Road, head southeast to the entry of the Water Canyon Campground and immediately bear right onto Cherry Canyon Trail. The narrow and rocky track hovers above the campground on the left. Soon after, the trail veers away from Water Canyon, and leads northwest across a sweeping marine terrace. And so begins a series of breathtaking island vistas.

After about a mile of easy hiking, bear left at a signed junction on Telephone Road, your path to Black Mountain. From here, climb along a rocky route through oak woodlands. With no obstructions to the views, panoramas are astounding. On clear days, take in the enormity of Bechers Bay, the

Torrey Pine Forest and Skunk Point to the east, and Carrington Point to the northeast. Gaze eastward at volatile Santa Cruz Passage with its unpredictable winds and swirling currents, separating Santa Rosa and Santa Cruz islands.

Continue southward to meet Soledad Road. Cross over the dirt road and continue almost 0.5 mile to the summit of Black Mountain and gain grand vistas of San Miguel Island to the northwest.

To return, you can retrace your steps, or make this into a loop hike by descending Soledad Road to the marine terraces above Bechers Bay, then back to the pier.

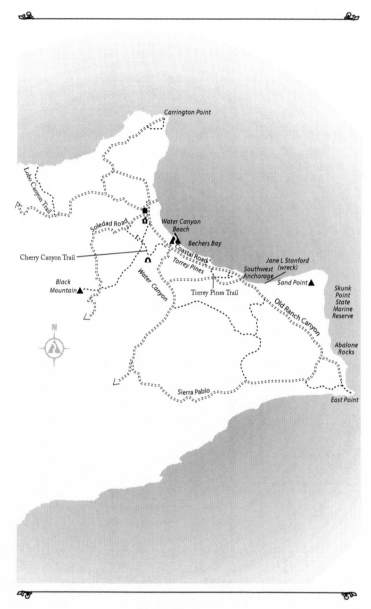

Carrington Point

Lobo Canyon Trail

Soledad Road

Water Canyon Beach

Cherry Canyon Trail

Bechers Bay

Coastal Road

Torrey Pines

Jane L Stanford (wreck)

Southwest Anchorage

Sand Point ▲

Skunk Point State Marine Reserve

Black Mountain▲

Water Canyon

Torrey Pines Trail

Old Ranch Canyon

Abalone Rocks

N

Sierra Pablo

East Point

Skunk Point and East Point

Coastal Road, Torrey Pines Trails

From Water Canyon Campground to Skunk Point is 8 miles round trip; to East Point is 13.5 miles round trip with 350-foot gain

Stunning views of Bechers Bay, Skunk Point, and the rugged southwest shore of Santa Rosa Island is a key attraction of the long hike to aptly named East Point, easternmost point on the island.

The usual route to East Point begins at Water Canyon Campground joins Coastal Road, following it past Skunk Point and the Southeast Anchorage until the road/trail dead ends at the point. During the winter-spring rainy seasons sections of the road tend to wash out and it can be a wet and mucky slog.

The trek to East Point is an all-day or most-of-a-day adventure. Skunk Point, easily visible from the pier, looks like it *could* be hiked while on a day trip to Santa Rosa. Actually, once you hit the beach and start that long slog in soft sand, the hike to Skunk Point, too, takes too long to accomplish on a day trip to the island.

Extending about 2.5 miles from Skunk Point to just short of East Point, Skunk Point State Marine Reserve protects a unique ocean ecosystem in a location where cold-water currents from Alaska and warm water currents from the tropics meet. A rocky reef and kelp forest, along with surfgrass and sandy sea floor, combine to host a wide variety of marine life. The reserve's Abalone Rocks is a nesting site for resident waterfowl and resting site for migratory birds.

Santa Rosa Island is the only island in the national park where backcountry beach camping is permitted, so you could make this hike a backpacking trip by planning for an overnight and some primitive camping on the bluffs overlooking East Point or nearby beaches. Backcountry camping is open from September 16–December 31. For backcountry permits, call 877-444-6777 or visit recreation.gov.

The beaches between Skunk Point 4 miles south to East Point are closed between March 1–September 15 to any kind of activity due to nesting western snowy plovers, a federally listed, threatened shorebird. You'll need to walk on the wet sand (below mean high tide) or on the road throughout this area.

DIRECTIONS: Begin at Water Canyon Campground.

THE HIKE: From the entrance to Water Canyon Campground, head southeast along Coastal Road, crossing over the year-round stream of Water Canyon that flows to the beach. From the narrow foot bridge, hike on the Coastal Road toward the Torrey Pine Forest.

Follow Coastal Road beneath the Torrey Pines Forest. Once past the forest, leave the Coastal Road behind and join a single track, keeping left atop a weather-beaten bluff leading toward the beach and Skunk Point.

The trail leads up steep sandy switchbacks to an old ranching double track with more mesmerizing vistas, this time of gritty Skunk Point. The long,

You can't miss Skunk Point with its long sweeping stretch of white sand.

sandy finger of Skunk Point is home to nesting western snowy plovers, a flotsam of splintered driftwood, and the *Jane L. Stanford* shipwreck, its remnants still protruding out of the constantly shifting sands of this deserted beach. The four-masted lumber schooner converted to a fishing barge was rammed by a mail steamer in 1929. Hardy shorebirds roost and nest in the ship's remains.

Beyond that pearly white sandy beach is the always unpredictable Santa Cruz Passage, and the rugged west end of Santa Cruz Island. The contrast of peaceful Skunk Point against one of the most volatile passages in the world is striking from this vantage point.

Continue south hiking toward a tranquil freshwater marsh, a convenient pitstop for migratory birds (some blown off course) during their spring and fall migrations. The trail continues meandering southward before rejoining the Coastal Road. Enjoy nearly continuous views of Santa Cruz Island to the east.

East Point teems with marine life. From atop the wave-battered bluffs, look down on the pocket beaches, perfect haul out sites for northern elephant seals, harbor seals and California sea lions. The creatures bask on these secluded beaches and out of those ever-present northwest winds.

At low tides the exposed reefs attract black oystercatchers, western gulls and Brandt's and pelagic cormorants making fishing forays into the intertidal zone. Keep an eye out for dolphins and the occasional whale just offshore.

Return the way you came or, if you're a super-motivated hiker looking for a 20-mile day, trek Sierra Pablo Road up the ridge overlooking the isle's southern coast of the island to meet South Road, which heads northeast back to Coast Road and the campground.

The hike to East Point is a splendid all-day adventure.

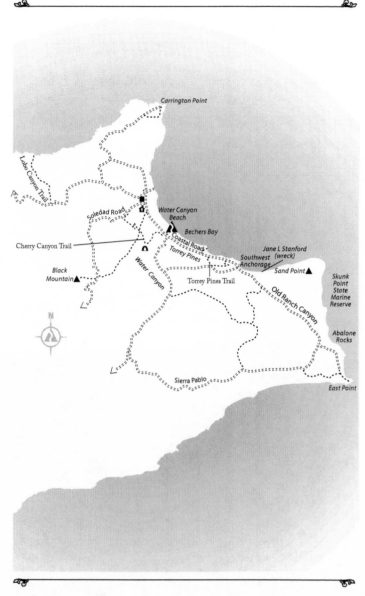

Carrington Point

Lobo Canyon Trail

Soledad Road

Water Canyon
Beach

Cherry Canyon Trail

Bechers Bay

Coastal Road

Torrey Pines

Jane L Stanford
(wreck)

Southwest
Anchorage

Sand Point

Skunk
Point
State
Marine
Reserve

Black
Mountain

Water Canyon

Torrey Pines Trail

Old Ranch Canyon

Abalone
Rocks

N

Sierra Pablo

East Point

TheTrailmaster.com

LOBO CANYON

SMITH ROAD, LOBO CANYON TRAIL

9 miles round trip with 400-foot elevation elevation gain

The trek through magical Lobo Canyon makes The Trailmaster's list of "Top Five Hikes in Southern California."

Over thousands of years the erosive power of wind and water have sculpted the stunning sandstone walls of Cañada Lobos, where native flora flourishes, including island monkey flower, dudleya and coreopsis. You'll likely see—and hear—plenty of tree frogs in the creek.

The upper part of Lobos Canyon is unexpectedly lush with coastal live oak draped with Spanish moss, a year-round creek and even the occasional banana slug. It's an even wetter and wilder hiking experience if you happen to hike the canyon in the morning fog with the dew dripping off the trees and plants and spider webs glistening with strings of dewy pearls.

Of course, if it's REALLY foggy, say with visibility of 150 to 200 feet or so, you'll feel like you're walking on another planet.

"But wait, there's more," as the infomercials say. At the mouth of the canyon is a lovely cove with a white sand beach.

Getting to the canyon takes a little doing. It's a labor and not exactly a labor of love to walk Smith Highway, a dirt road with a modest but relentless ascent that extends from the coast to the trailhead at the head of Lobo Canyon.

DIRECTIONS: Island Packers runs regular boat trips to Santa Rosa.

THE HIKE: From the landing pier, walk inland toward the red barn. Behind it is your trailhead for this hike—the start of Smith Road, which extends toward Lobo Canyon. After crossing Water Canyon, the road begins to climb, and you can get over the shoulder views of the ranch buildings, Bechers Bay, and the Torrey pine forest.

About 1.25 mile from the trailhead, reach a grassy expanse known as Carrington Pasture and a junction with the road that leads toward Carrington Point, where the remains of the long extinct Channel Island pygmy mammoth were discovered in 1994.

Continue ascending along Smith Highway and, about 3 miles along, arrive at the edge of Lobo

Canyon. The road descends to a little picnic area under the oaks and the signed trailhead.

Now the real fun begins. The path meanders through a riparian corridor lined with tall toyon, cattails, willows, and cottonwood. What a big difference a little water makes!

Reaching the upper section of the canyon, you walk along narrow planks across the marshy canyon bottom and gaze up at the high walls rising above.

You'll hear the roar of the breakers a good bit before you spot the cove. Trail's end is a nearly always deserted white sand beach. Enjoy a picnic, take a dip (if it's not too cold and windy), and enjoy views of the mainland and west toward San Miguel Island.

Lobo Canyon Trail's dramatic end at a lovely cove and beach.

The epic hike to Point Bennett leads to the planet's largest congregation of seals and sea lions.

EVERY TRAIL TELLS A STORY.

IV
SAN MIGUEL
ISLAND

HIKE ON.

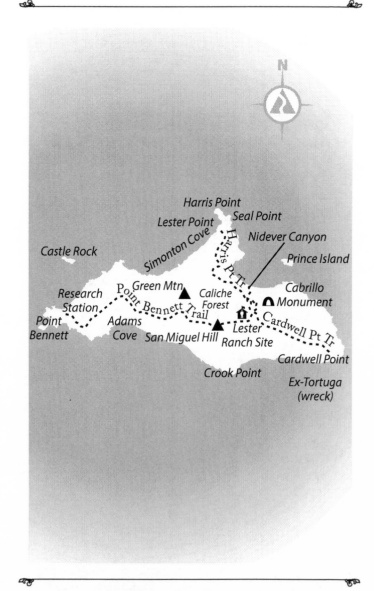

N

Harris Point
Lester Point
Seal Point
Simonton Cove
Nidever Canyon
Castle Rock
Prince Island
Green Mtn.
Caliche Forest
Cabrillo Monument
Research Station
Point Bennett Trail
Point Bennett
Adams Cove
San Miguel Hill
Lester Ranch Site
Cardwell Pt Tr.
Cardwell Point
Crook Point
Ex-Tortuga (wreck)

Cuyler Harbor & Nidever Canyon

Nidever Canyon Trail

From Cuyler Harbor to Ranger Station is 3 miles round trip with 700-feet elevation gain

Cuyler Harbor is arguably the most scenic natural harbor in Channel Islands National Park.

In some visitors' eyes, the long curvy beach at Cuyler Harbor, with Prince Island as a perfect backdrop, resembles a secluded beach in the South Pacific.

The harbor was named after the original government surveyor in the 1850s. The beach around the anchorage was formed by a bight of volcanic cliffs that extend to bold and precipitous Harris Point, one of the most prominent landmarks on San Miguel's coast.

More of a massive rock outcropping than an island, Prince Island offers ideal nesting habitat for 13 seabird species including hardy Cassin's auklets, pigeon guillemots, common murres, California brown pelicans, western gulls, ashy storm petrels and other seafaring species. The 40-acre island hosts the most diverse seabird colony on the West Coast.

The steep hike from the beach by Cuyler Harbor, up Nidever Canyon to the ranger station is the only hike on San Miguel that is not ranger escorted. So you can visit a few major sights on your own, including Cabrillo Monument and the Lester Ranch site.

DIRECTIONS: Expect a 3- to 4-hour boat ride—depending on sea conditions and wildlife sightings—to San Miguel Island. Island Packers drops anchor in the protected harbor, and from there the crew transports visitors by skiff to a sandy beach.

THE HIKE: Once visitors touch down on the beach next to wave-battered Gull Rock, there's no missing the wind-sculpted, pearly-white sand dunes beneath the steep cliffs at the bottom of Nidever Canyon. Follow the trail into the dunes and the narrow single track hugging the left side of the canyon. You'll pass a trickling spring on the right side.

The winding ascent through Nidever Canyon is a botanist's dream. Come springtime, dense stocks of vibrant Indian paintbrush, daisy-like coreopsis, island poppies and buckwheat brighten the rugged canyon.

About halfway up the canyon you'll reach a T-intersection. Head left, and to the southeast, toward the Juan Rodriguez Cabrillo Monument. Cabrillo was a Portuguese explorer sailing under the Spanish flag. In 1542 he was the first European to set foot on what is now California and the Channel Islands. He was also the first European to have contact with the resident Chumash Indians on the archipelago.

Just before the campground, bear right to the Lester Ranch Site. Herbert Lester, wife Elizabeth and daughters, Marianne and Betsy lived on the isle from 1930 to 1942. Herbert Lester ran a sheep ranch and gained celebrity status as the self-proclaimed "King of San Miguel." Newspapers portrayed Lester as living a sort of "Hemingwayesque" lifestyle on the rugged island.

When a ranger is present, you can stop by the visitor center at the ranger station. Restrooms are located at the campground and ranger station.

A narrow footpath leads to a plethora of native flora in Nidever Canyon.

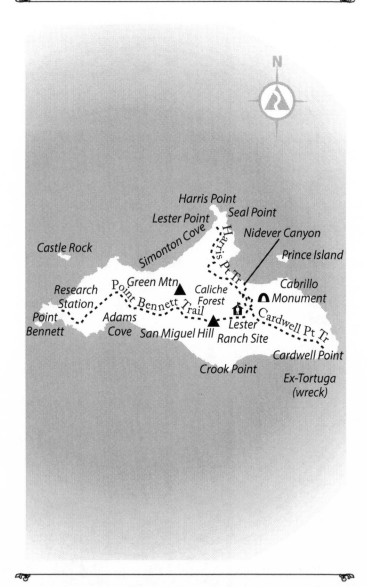

N

Harris Point

Lester Point

Seal Point

Simonton Cove

Nidever Canyon

Castle Rock

Harris Pt Tr

Prince Island

Research Station

Point Bennett Trail

Green Mtn

Caliche Forest

Cabrillo Monument

Point Bennett

Adams Cove

San Miguel Hill

Lester Ranch Site

Cardwell Pt Tr

Crook Point

Cardwell Point

Ex-Tortuga (wreck)

HARRIS POINT

From the campground to Harris Point is 6.2 miles round trip.

Virtually the entire hike to the northern tip of the island and Harris Point offers breathtaking views: Nidever Canyon, Cuyler Harbor, Prince Island, Simonton Cove, Castle Rock and eventually the overlook above wave-battered Harris Point.

A large promontory on the north side of the island, Harris Point forms the western headland and protection for Cuyler's Harbor. Northwest winds and swell hammer away at all the exposed rocky crags of the point which is cloaked in multi-colored lichen, San Miguel Island live-forever, buckwheat, and other hardy native plants.

This hike is an awesome one at sunset. As the sun dips just beyond Castle Rock to the west, the rugged beauty of Harris Point becomes amplified. (Don't forget your headlamp for the walk back in the dark.)

DIRECTIONS: Ranger-led hike to Harris Point begin at the Ranger Station.

THE HIKE: This hike typically begins in the campground and descends Nidever Canyon. After several hundred yards of northward travel, you reach a junction. The single track to the right descends back to the beach at Cuyler Harbor. Our route heads north to the site of the original two-room, plywood ranger station that was nestled in Nidever Canyon. Now it's the location of a water-pumping station, one of the few year-round springs on the island.

After crossing the streambed, the trail descends the canyon to the site of the old adobe homestead of canyon namesake George Nidever. Nidever was a skilled frontiersman, as well as a seafaring captain and homesteader in Santa Barbara.

The trail hugs the bluffs overlooking Cuyler Harbor and Prince Island, which lies about a half mile offshore. Prince Island is a vital seabird nesting site for Cassin's auklets, common murres, pelagic cormorants, western gulls and other hardy species.

Keep an eye out for enormous northern elephant seals basking on deserted beaches. Listen for bellowing California sea lions that share the sand below the steep bluffs. This is one of the most epic seascapes across the entire northern chain of islands.

The trail continues along the edge of the bluff then soon veers inland over a marine terrace cloaked in bushels of buckwheat, fragrant bush lupine and vibrant island poppies.

Hike north to vistas of the long and exposed Simonton Cove and beyond it the tall sea stack known as Castle Rock. Northwesterly winds can increase without warning on this exposed stretch of the hike as it continues along a sandy stretch over the marine terrace. Beyond this broad plateau is a gradual ridge that leads to two peaks on a headland. A short distance farther, a path leads to an overlook about 300 feet above sea level and reveals the stunning beach tucked inside the craggy finger of Harris Point.

Harris Point has had its share of tragedy, too. To the east is the burial site of Herbert Lester and his wife Betsy. Lester operated a sheep ranch on the island from 1930 to 1942. Also known as "the King of San Miguel", he was despondent when he received word that the U.S. Navy wanted him off the island. He committed suicide and was buried at what is now known as Lester Point overlooking Harris Point. His wife Betsy passed away in 1981 and was buried next to her husband.

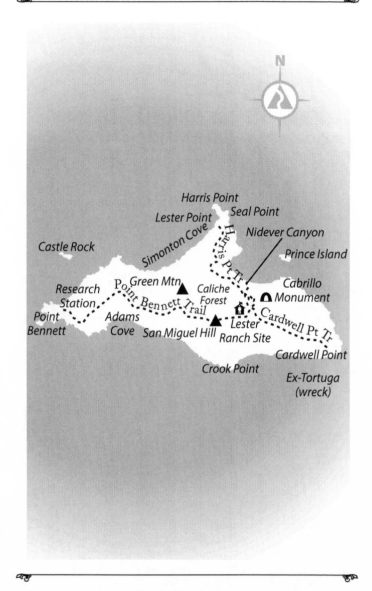

CROOK POINT

CROOK POINT OVERLOOK TRAIL

From Cuyler Harbor to Crook Point Overlook is 5 miles round-trip; from the Ranger Station it's 3.5 miles round-trip

Fresh off the Island Packers ferry, if it's an easy ranger-led day hike you're looking for, consider the hike to the sweeping overlook at Crook Point. It's a great preview for what hiking will be like on San Miguel Island.

To repeat: More than any other island, San Miguel is exposed to rapidly changing weather conditions. Even on a short hike like this one, hikers may face high winds and thick fog blowing over the island at any moment

If on a day trip via Island Packers, the hike will begin at Cuyler Harbor. Because the hike from Cuyler Harbor, through the sand dunes, up Nidever Canyon, and to the ranger station can be hiked on your own, the ranger on island may elect to meet hikers at the ranger station. If you're camping, you'll walk over to the ranger station to join the guided hike.

DIRECTIONS: Meet up at the ranger station to begin this escorted hike.

THE HIKE: The route briefly follows the air strip east of the ranger station. Enjoy fantastic clear-day views of the northwest end of Santa Rosa Island and even the northwest end of Santa Cruz Island. (btw, air strip adjacent vistas at sunrise are truly epic.)

The trail meanders across mostly flat terrain. (It shares the same beginnings as the Cardwell Point hike. See description.) After 0.5 mile, the trail forks to the right and southeast through clusters of San Miguel Island liveforever, bushels of coyote bush, and San Miguel Island buckwheat.

Pass several chain-link pens that remain from the years when island foxes were captive bred by wildlife biologists determined to bring the animals back from the edge of extinction. The island fox was placed on the Endangered Species List in 2002. The team from Channel Islands National Park, The Nature Conservancy and Institute for Wildlife Studies did a masterful job of rearing island foxes and increasing their population to a point that in 2016, the fox was delisted—no longer considered an endangered species. The pens remain behind just in case some calamity arises that prompts the breeding program to be revived.

From the pens, it's an easy, gradual descent to the overlook. Hikers are greeted with incredible views of Crook Point and its many tranquil pocket beaches, frequented by northern elephant seals lazily sunning the day away. Listen for the bellowing and barking of California sea lions, hauled-out on the shores below.

Marine scientists have been monitoring the inner and outer reefs of Crook Point since 1985. Biodiversity surveys focus on such marker species as California mussel, acorn barnacle and golden rockweed.

Train your field glasses on the throngs of seabirds swooping offshore and roosting on this remote coastline's craggy outposts and scan the airways for peregrine falcons soaring overhead.

On the hike to Crook Point bring field glasses to view elephant seals and throngs of seabirds.

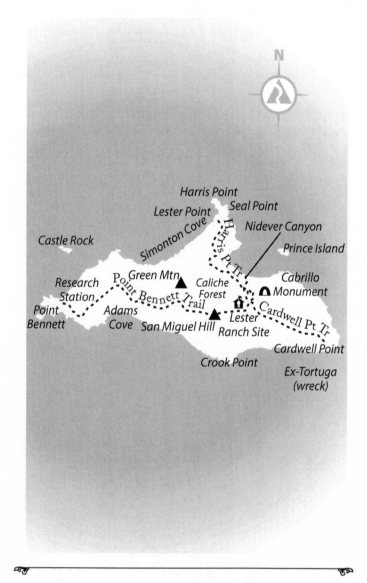

N

Harris Point

Lester Point   Seal Point

Simonton Cove   Nidever Canyon

Castle Rock   Prince Island

Research   Green Mtn.   Caliche   Cabrillo
Station   Point Bennett Trail   Forest   Monument

Point   Adams   Cardwell Pt Tr
Bennett   Cove   San Miguel Hill   Lester
                                        Ranch Site

                                        Cardwell Point

Crook Point

Ex-Tortuga
(wreck)

TheTrailmaster.com

CARDWELL POINT

From Ranger Station to Cardwell Point is 6 miles round trip

As a pinniped-viewing locale, Cardwell Point tends to get overlooked because the creatures can conveniently be seen from the beach at Cuyler Harbor and because the West Coast's most famous and diverse pinniped viewing location is at Point Bennett.

Our strong recommendation: Don't overlook the hike to Cardwell Point Overlook.

The moderate hike to Cardwell Point on the eastern tip of San Miguel is well worth the effort. About halfway across the island, you'll hear something that'll spur you on, and encourage your feet to keep moving. That something is a sound—faint at first, but gradually getting louder and louder. The noise is a sort of rumble, low and rolling, more like a knock like using your tongue on the roof of your mouth.

What can be making this strange sound?

As you come over the rise at Cardwell Point you find your answer: dozens of elephant seals on the beach—flipping sand over their huge torpedo-shaped bodies, moving like globs of JELLO over the sand, and carving out territories to call their own. The originators of the noise you've been listening to are the gigantic males with their long proboscises that give the species its name.

Cardwell Point's dramatic bluffs are advantageous perches for pelagic and Brandt's cormorants clinging to and waiting for the next bait ball of fish to arrive, carried by the continuous ebb and flow of tides and currents surrounding the point.

DIRECTIONS: Hikes to Cardwell Point begin at the ranger station and are ranger-led. Don't forget your field glasses.

THE HIKE Heading southeast on the airstrip, you'll be escorted on a narrow single-track trail through massive clusters of San Miguel Island live-forevers and sprawling coyote bush, and across non-native grassland dotted with giant coreopsis, lupine, and dudleya.

Keep an eye out for elusive island foxes. The foxes on San Miguel tend to be less outgoing than their foxy counterparts on Santa Cruz Island.

After two short descents into seasonal arroyos, the path leads downhill toward the exposed overlook at Cardwell Point. Once there, observe the open ocean expanse that is San Miguel Passage. It's three miles southeast across the passage to the gnarled, wave-battered fingers and pocket beaches of Sandy Point and the northwest end of Santa Rosa Island.

Usually, you'll spot a few northern elephant seals wallowing on the beach and lazily swimming in the shallows at high tide at the base of the bluff. Also, gaze out at Nichols Point, a quarter mile to the northeast. A small sandspit beach there is a favorite haul out site for California sea lions.

The wildlife watching doesn't end here though. You'll be escorted a short distance to the west to another overlook revealing throngs of sea lions and first-year northern elephant seals occupying a wind-blown beach backed by a steep sand dune at the base of a sheer cliff. (Hikers will need to stay low on the approach and sit at all times while taking in the drama of the highly concentrated pinniped rookery.) The sights, sounds and, yes, smells (!) of the animals are memorable to say the least.

During solid south swells, look for groups of sea lions bodysurfing onto the crowded beach; the sea lions ride the surf, then are flung up onto the wet sand by frothy whitewater. Apparently their enthusiasm knows no bounds as they hurry back out to the pounding surf to catch another wave.

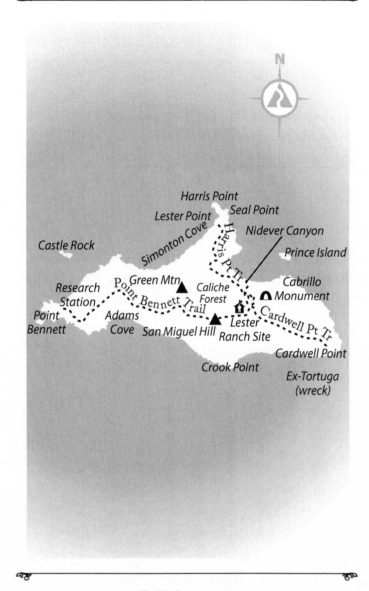

N

Harris Point
Lester Point
Seal Point
Simonton Cove
Nidever Canyon
Harris Pt Tr.
Castle Rock
Prince Island
Green Mtn.
Caliche Forest
Cabrillo Monument
Research Station
Point Bennett Trail
Cardwell Pt. Tr.
Point Bennett
Adams Cove
San Miguel Hill
Lester Ranch Site
Cardwell Point
Crook Point
Ex-Tortuga (wreck)

TheTrailmaster.com

POINT BENNETT

From Ranger Station to Point Bennett is 14 miles round trip with 500-foot elevation gain

If we had to choose a one-word description of the hike to Point Bennett, it would be "epic."

The hike extends across most of the length of the island to its western tip, the westernmost point of Channel Islands National Park. Along the way, the trail leads past the island's two round peaks— San Miguel and Green Mountain—and travels to the Caliche Forest, composed of fossil sand casts of ancient plants and trees. Beyond this moonscape, at trail's end, is Point Bennett and the largest congregation of seals and sea lions in the world. Epic indeed!

This "once in a lifetime" hike is ranger-led only. However, on the return, hikers are free to walk back on their own.

DIRECTIONS: To take this hike, you'll need to camp a minimum of two nights on San Miguel

Island. You'll meet the ranger in the morning at the ranger station for the escorted hike to Point Bennett.

THE HIKE: Beginning at the airstrip, you'll connect with the trailhead shortly after leaving the ranger station. Heading west, the trail makes a gradual ascent of San Miguel Hill (elevation 831 feet). After passing by a weather apparatus, and about 1.5 miles from the ranger station, the path meets a short (0.2 mile) connector trail that leads to the Caliche Forest, truly one of the most unique natural wonders in Channel Islands National Park.

The ghostly forest was created when calcium carbonate reacted with the trees' organic acid. What

A ghostly forest like no other, the Caliche Forest is a collection of casts of trees that disappeared eons ago.

remains are the calcified stumps of what may be an ancient grove of cypress and pine trees. According to the National Park Service, one casting measures 30 feet long and is 2 feet in diameter.

Back on the main trail, hikers continue west toward Green Mountain (elevation 817 feet). The trail

Point Bennett, the edge of the world—or at least the westernmost point of the Channel Islands.

meanders along on the east face of the mount and delivers stupendous clear-day views of Santa Rosa Island's southwest shore.

Next comes a gradual descent to the dry lake region of the island, and to an airstrip utilized by biologists of the research station overlooking Point Bennett. From the airstrip, the trail leads southwest, rolls along, ascends onto a weathered section of the isle where nothing seems to thrive, then voilà the first views of Point Bennett!

The pinniped symphony increases as you draw closer to the research station, a good spot to take in the wildlife spectacle below. A long gritty beach extends west and beyond to a smattering of exposed reefs and wave-battered rock outcroppings. Real estate is at a premium at Point Bennett as six different species of pinnipeds breed, pup and haul out here: California sea lions, northern fur seals, harbor seals, northern elephant seals, Guadalupe fur seals and Steller sea lions.

From the research facility, hikers make a gradual descent to the sand dunes overlooking Adams Cove and the beach extending to Point Bennett. When there's a south swell there's a lot of good bodysurfing going on as young fur seals and sea lions ride the shore-pound up a steep berm to their basking counterparts. Other drama on the beach includes nursing pups, squabbles over territory, and young pups playing and jousting in the tide pools.

Not many of us get to experience a wildlife drama like this, a hike like this. We count ourselves fortunate, and hope you do, too.

Some seals and sea lions sun themselves on the sandy beach while others go body-surfing at Point Bennett.

Welcome to Santa Barbara Island,
home to scores of sea lions and cormorants.

EVERY TRAIL TELLS A STORY.

V
SANTA BARBARA
ISLAND

HIKE ON.

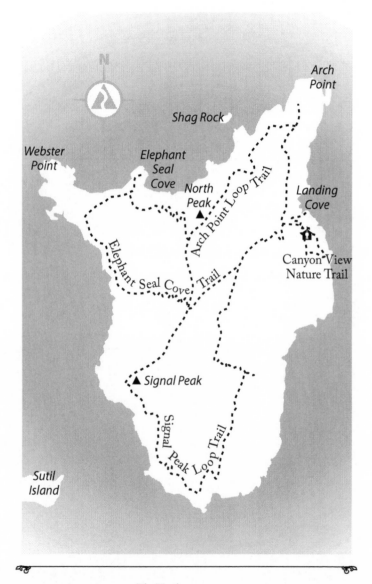

Arch
Point

Shag Rock

Webster
Point

Elephant
Seal
Cove

North
Peak

Landing
Cove

Arch Point Loop Trail

Canyon View
Nature Trail

Elephant Seal Cove Trail

Signal Peak

Signal Peak Loop Trail

Sutil
Island

TheTrailmaster.com

Santa Barbara Island

Loop Trails

Signal Peak Loop is 3 miles round trip with 600-foot elevation gain; Arch Point-Elephant Seal Cove Loop is 4 miles round trip with 500-foot gain.

Only one square mile in area, Santa Barbara Island is the smallest of California's Channel Island. It's located some 38 miles west of San Pedro—or quite a bit south of the other islands in the national park. Since it's so small, it can only be seen from the mainland on rare occasions—usually on very clear winter days, in silhouette at sunset.

Geologically speaking, Santa Barbara Island arose a bit differently from the other isles. The island is a volcano, leftover from Miocene times, some 25 million years ago, and shares characteristics with Mexico's Guadalupe Islands.

Explorer Sebastian Vizcaino sailed by on December 4, 1602. That day happened to be the day of remembrance for Saint Barbara, so the island was named for her. In 1938 Santa Barbara Island was preserved as a national monument, then included in the newly established Channel Islands National Park in 1980.

From a distance, the triangular-shaped island looks barren—not a tree in sight. Closer, you might see bright yellow bouquets of the coreopsis, the giant tree sunflower that can grow 10-feet high. Other springtime bloomers such as cream cups, shrubby buckwheat and Santa Barbara Island live-forever splash color across the isle.

To birdwatchers, Santa Barbara means seabirds, 11 nesting species including cormorants, pelicans, and black oystercatchers plus western gulls by the thousands. And the island boasts some rare birds, too: the black storm-petrel and the Xantus murrelet. Land birds commonly sighted include burrowing and barn owls, hummingbirds, horned larks and house finches. Brown boobies now nest on Sutil Island, located a very short distance south of Santa Barbara Island.

The isle's native plants and wildlife suffered greatly from early 20th century ranching, farming and hunting activities. Thanks to the National Park Service's restoration efforts, however, native vegetation is once again flourishing which, in turn, has greatly boosted the return of nesting birds.

Trails lead to overlooks of Elephant Seal Cove, Webster Point and Sea Lion Rookery where you gaze down at the seals and barking sea lions. Webster Point on the western end of the isle is a favorite haul-out area for the pinnipeds.

DIRECTIONS: Public boat trips for park visitors are generally limited to a few days each month during the summer. However, as of this writing, the Santa Barbara Island Dock is closed and there are no commercial boat trips scheduled to the island by national park concessionaire, Island Packers. Check with the National Park Service about the status of the dock, heavily damaged by a series of storms in 2017, and unlikely to be repaired in the near future. The island is open to public access if you can arrange private transport, with landings restricted to a rocky ledge adjacent to the dock.

THE HIKE Once you hike the short steep trail from the Landing Cove up the rugged cliffs, you'll find more than five miles of trail crisscrossing the island. A good place to start your exploration is Canyon View Nature Trail.

Thirty or so midden sites (piles of broken shells) suggest use of the island by native peoples may date back 4,000 years. Hikers will notice particularly large middens on the trail to Arch Point and along the saddle between North and Signal peaks.

On the Signal Peak loop, you'll get great views of the island and a whole lot of Pacific from island high points North Peak (562 feet) and Signal Peak (635 feet).

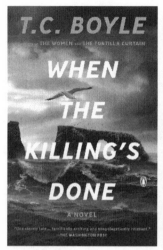 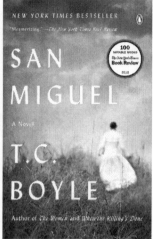

T.C. Boyle's *When the Killing's Done* (2011) features Channel Islands National Park biologist Alma Boyd Takesue in her battle to save native species by eliminating invasive ones. She faces off with Dave LaJoy, a local businessman and animal rights activist opposed to killing any animals and will stop at nothing to subvert her plans.

Boyle's *San Miguel* (2013) is set on San Miguel Island and focuses on two troubled families—one in the 1880s and one in the 1930s—who come to the isle for a new start in their lives. Particularly fascinating is this fictional account of the real-life Lester family as seen through the eyes of Elise Lester, married to Herbert Lester, the so-called "King of San Miguel" and her hardships raising two daughters in harsh isolation.

CHANNEL ISLAND STORIES

HIKE ON.

The Channel Islands of California

Charles Frederick Holder (1851-1915) was an American naturalist, conservationist, and writer who penned more than 40 books and thousands of articles. *The Channel Islands of California: A Book for the Angler, Sportsman, and Tourist* was published in 1910. This excerpt is from a chapter about Santa Cruz Island, "The Island of the Sacred Cross."

It is said that Cabrillo often entered Prisoners Harbor in Santa Cruz. Above the anchorage the island mountains rose, tier after tier, covered here and there with a thick growth of pine, manzanita, and other trees, from which waved filaments and pennants of moss.

We waited on the pier, where a large sign gave notice that intruders were not wanted. It so happened that we had letters to the owner, Justinian Caire, which insured us welcome to the island, and to one of the most picturesque ranches on the Pacific Coast. From the sea, Santa Cruz Island is a jumble of lofty hills and mountains, with deep gorges and cañons winding in every direction. Hidden away in the very heart of this island is an ideal ranch.

The Caire Ranch has been in existence for nearly thirty years; but probably it has not been heard of in the East and is known by few people on the Pacific Coast. Yet here on an island twenty miles out in the Pacific, up a cañon almost impassable at times in winter, is a model ranch, presided over by its superintendent and attended to by sixty or more men. The proprietor is French, and French and Italian laborers are employed exclusively, the original plan having been to establish here a Swiss-French colony. The little valley in the interior and its climate, so similar to that of Italy and Southern France, probably inspired the owner to reproduce a European vineyard here, and so faithfully has the idea been carried out that on entering the valley one can easily imagine himself in one of the wine-producing districts of France or Italy.

There are two distinctive seasons at the Santa Cruz Island ranch—the sheep-shearing and the vintage, when the French and Italian islanders are reinforced by the Barbareños, from Santa Barbara, who pick the grapes in September and shear the sheep twice a year. The latter work requires men of this hardy stock and the finest horsemen, and probably in no other country are men seen riding over such inaccessible mountains. The sheep, of which there are thirty thousand or more, range all over the fifty-six thousand acres of the island, except in the valley in the interior, devoted to the ranch and vineyard.

In climate this island compares most favorably with any part of the Riviera, as here are none of the hot winds of Africa or the cold breezes from the Maritime Alps. The air is clear, pure, "delicioso." Surely this is the land of *dolce far niente* [pleasant idleness].

Report on San Miguel Island (NPS)

In 1957 the National Park Service published its "Report on San Miguel Island of the Channel Islands, California," suggesting San Miguel would be a worthy addition to Channel Islands National Monument, which then included Anacapa and Santa Barbara islands. Despite the report writers' enthusiasm, San Miguel would not come under NPS protection until 1980.

The principal known values of San Miguel Island include an extensive region of unspoiled scenic ocean beaches, a unique and enthralling springtime display of wildflowers, now recovering from a history of past grazing, and a truly outstanding display of wildlife. The herds of elephant seals, sea lions, of two species of sea otters, and the remarkably tame San Miguel foxes, are unique. These, together with the great rookeries of nesting sea birds, and the several pairs of nesting American eagles are in need of absolute protection by a qualified governmental body.

One obvious need for conservation at San Miguel Island is that for some seventy years it was so abused through grazing activities that many thought it was literally and hopelessly blowing away into the sea. Now completely devoid of human habitation, San Miguel is a place where the flora and fauna, unique and ordinary alike are free to recover from the ravages of past human occupation and use.

While it may not appear at this time that large scale visitation by the general public would be very heavy to San Miguel in the immediate future the outlook may well be utterly different. Aside from observations of scenery, wildlife and scientific resources of the island it appears some twenty-four miles of clean, unspoiled beaches will have much to offer simply for rest and relaxation, provided adequate protection can be assured for the natural features of the island.

A growing number of recreation visitors are attracted by the good anchorage at Cuyler Harbor, the beaches and wildlife. There is a wilderness appeal that the amateur photographer and explorer enjoys. Comparatively few people know anything about San Miguel so far, however, and few other than fishermen and yachtsmen have ever been there. But this situation, the reporters believe, will not last for many more years.

It is believed that the National Park Service would be justified in recommending the addition to Channel Islands National Monument of San Miguel Island and its immediate surroundings, including an area one nautical mile out from the mean tide level of the island.

Island of the Blue Dolphins

Island of the Blue Dolphins is a 1960 children's novel by Scott O'Dell, which tells the story of a 12-year-old girl named Karana stranded alone on an island off the California coast.

The tale, much beloved by generations of elementary and middle school students, is fascinating for its portrayal of Karana's relationship with nature—land, sea, fish, animals—and an island that is at once beautiful and terrifying.

The novel is a work of historical fiction based on the true story of a Nicoleño Native Californian woman left alone for 18 years on San Nicholas Island. "The Lone Woman of San Nicholas Island," as she was known, was discovered and taken back to the mainland in 1853 by explorer-sea otter hunter George Nidever.

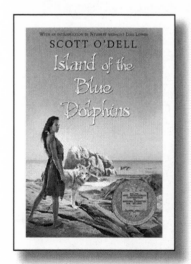

An award-winning classic novel for children: "Island of the Blue Dolphins."

Tragically, no one alive at that time spoke her language and we have no record of her name or anything about her life. Estimated to be about 50 years old, she was given the name Juana Maria by the padres at the Santa Barbara Mission, where she was buried just 7 weeks after being removed from the island.

Today, the U.S. Navy owns San Nicolas Island and it's closed to visitors, but you can get an "Island of the Blue Dolphins" experience on the five Channel Islands that are part of the national park.

The Lone Woman of San Nicolas Island depicted as she may have looked in 1853 by the artist Holli Harmon.

Death Valley NP
YOSEMITE NATIONAL PARK
LAVA BEDS NM
César Chávez NM
Pinnacles National Park
EUGENE O'NEIL NHS
MUIR WOODS NM
Whiskeytown-Shasta Trinity NRA
Joshua Tree National Recreation Area
Golden Gate National Recreation Area
DEVILS POSTPILE NM
LASSEN VOLCANIC NATIONAL PARK
Death Valley NP
REDWOOD NP
CHANNEL ISLANDS NATIONAL PARK
Cabrillo NM
LAVA BEDS NM
Joshua Tree National Park
YOSEMITE NATIONAL PARK
MOJAVE NPRES
MUIR WOODS NM
César Chávez NM
John Muir NHS
Rosie the Riveter NHS
Santa Monica Mountains NRA
LASSEN VOLCANIC NATIONAL PARK
YOSEMITE NATIONAL PARK
MOJAVE NPRES
Rosie the Riveter NHS
Death Valley NP
Cabrillo NM
Pinnacles NP
POINT REYES NS
John Muir NHS
SEQUOIA - KINGS CANYON NATIONAL PARKS
EUGENE O'NEIL NHS
DEVILS POSTPILE NM
POINT REYES NS
Whiskeytown-Shasta Trinity NRA

CALIFORNIA'S
NATIONAL PARKS

Other states have national parks with tall trees, high peaks, deep canyons, long seashores and vast deserts, but only California can claim all these grand landscapes within its boundaries.

California boasts nine national parks, the most in the nation. In addition, the state's national parklands include national recreation areas, national monuments, national historic parks, a national seashore and a national preserve.

The state features one of America's oldest national parks—Yosemite set aside in 1890—and one of its newest—César E. Chávez National Monument established in 2012.

Mere acreage does not a national park make, but California's national parks include the largest park in the contiguous U.S.—3.3-million acre Death Valley National Park. Yosemite (748,542 acres) and Joshua Tree (790,636 acres) are also huge by any park standards. Even such smaller parklands as Redwoods National Park and Pt. Reyes National Seashore are by no means small.

California and The National Park Idea

Not long after John Muir walked through Mariposa Grove and into the Yosemite Valley, California's natural treasures attracted attention worldwide and conservationists rallied to preserve them as parks. As the great naturalist put it in 1898: "Thousands of nerve-shaken, overcivilized people are beginning to find out that going to the mountains is going home; that wilderness is a necessity; and that mountain parks and reservations are useful not only as fountains of timber and irrigating rivers, but as fountains of life."

The National Park Service, founded in 1916, was initially guided by borax tycoon-turned-park-champion Stephen T. Mather and his young assistant, California attorney Horace Albright. The park service's mission was the preservation of "the scenery and the natural and historic objects and the wild life" and the provision "for the enjoyment of the same in such manner and by such means as will leave them unimpaired for the enjoyment of future generations."

The invention of the automobile revolutionized national park visitation, particularly in car-conscious California. John Muir called them "blunt-nosed mechanical beetles," yet as one California senator pointed out, "If Jesus Christ had an automobile he wouldn't have ridden a jackass into Jerusalem."

With cars came trailers, and with trailer camps came concessionaires. National parks filled with mobile cities of canvas and aluminum, and by visitors anxious to see California's natural wonders. During the 1920s and 30s, the park service constructed signs identifying scenic features and rangers assumed the role of interpreting nature for visitors.

By 1930 California had four national parks: Yosemite, Lassen, Sequoia and General Grant (Kings Canyon.) In the 1930s, two big desert areas—Joshua Tree and Death Valley—became national monuments.

With the 1960s came hotly contested, and eventually successful campaigns to create Redwood National

Steven Mather (R) and his assistant Horace Albright guided the National Park Service in its early days.

Park and Point Reyes National Seashore. During the 1970s the National Park Service established parks near the state's big cities—Golden Gate National Recreation Area on the San Francisco waterfront and Marin headlands and Santa Monica Mountains National Recreation Area, a Mediterranean ecosystem near Los Angeles. Also during that decade, Mineral King Valley was saved from a mega-ski resort development and added to Sequoia National Park. Channel Islands National Park, an archipelago offshore from Santa Barbara, was established in 1980.

During the 1980s and 1990s, major conservation battles raged in the desert. After more than two decades of wrangling, Joshua Tree and Death Valley national monuments were greatly expanded and given national park status, and the 1.6-million acre Mojave National Preserve was established under provisions of the 1994 California Desert Conservation Act.

Today, the National Park Service must address challenging questions: How best to regulate concessionaires? Should motor vehicles be banned from Yosemite Valley? How can aging park facilities cope with many years of deferred maintenance?

And the biggest issue of all: How will our parks (indeed our planet!) cope with the rapidly increasing effects of climate change?

The consequences of climate change to California's national parks is ever more apparent. In recent years, after prolonged droughts, devastating wildfires burned the Yosemite backcountry, parts of Sequoia National Park and more than half the Santa Monica Mountains National Recreation Area. Scientists have discovered that trees in Sequoia and Kings Canyon national parks endure the worst ozone levels of all national parks, in part because of their proximity to farm-belt air in the San Joaquin Valley.

California's national parklands struggle with an ever-increasing numbers of visitors. The California Office of Tourism charts visitation to national parks along with airports, hotel occupancy and other attractions such as Disneyland and Universal Studios. Yosemite is California's most-visited park with 4.5 to 5 million visitors a year, and many other parks count millions of visitors or "visitor days," per year.

What may be the saving grace of national parks is the deep-seated, multi-generational pride Americans have for their national parklands. We not only love national parks, we love the very idea of national parks. Even in an era of public mistrust toward government, national parks remain one of the most beloved institutions of American life.

National Parks have often been celebrated as America's best idea. As writer Wallace Stegner put it: "National parks are the best idea we ever had. Absolutely American, absolutely democratic, they reflect us at our best rather than our worst."

The Trails

The state of the state's national park trail system is excellent. Trailhead parking, interpretive panels and displays, as well as signage, is generally tops in the field. Backcountry junctions are usually signed and trail conditions, with a few exceptions of course, range from good to excellent.

Trail systems evolved on a park-by-park basis and it's difficult to speak in generalities about their respective origins. A good deal of Yosemite's trail system was in place before the early horseless carriages chugged into the park.

Several national parks were aided greatly by the Depression-era Civilian Conservation Corps of the 1930s. Sequoia and Pinnacles national parks, for example, have hand-built trails by the CCC that are true gems, highlighted by stonework and bridges that would no doubt be prohibitively expensive to construct today.

Scout troops, the hard-working young men and women of the California Conservation Corps and many volunteer groups are among the organizations that help park staff build and maintain trails.

The trail system in California's national parklands shares many characteristics in common with pathways overseen by other governmental bodies, and have unique qualities as well. One major difference between national parks and, for example, California's state parks, is the amount of land preserved as wilderness. A majority of Yosemite, Sequoia, Death Valley, Joshua Tree and several more parks are official federally designated wilderness. Wilderness comprises some 94 percent of Yosemite National Park, 93 percent of Death Valley National Park, and more than 80 percent of Joshua Tree National Park.

On national park maps you'll find wilderness areas delineated as simply "Wilderness." Unlike the Forest Service, the Bureau of Land Management or other wilderness stewards, the National Park Service does not name its wilderness areas.

Author John McKinney admires the sign for Yosemite's Four Mile Trail.

"Wilderness" is more than a name for a wild area. By law, a wilderness is restricted to non-motorized entry—that is to say, equestrian and foot travel. Happily, hikers do not have to share the trails with snowmobiles or mountain bikes in national park wilderness.

Because national park trails attract visitors from all over the globe, the park service makes use of international symbols on its signage, and the metric system as well. Don't be surprised if you spot trail signs with distance expressed in kilometers as well as miles and elevation noted in meters as well as feet.

The hikers you meet on a national park trail may be different from the company you keep on trails near home. California's national parks attract increasing numbers of ethnically and culturally diverse hikers of all ages, shapes and sizes, from across the nation and around the world. Once I counted ten languages on a popular trail in Yosemite! The hiking experience is much enriched by sharing the trail with hikers from literally all walks of life.

California's National Parklands

Alcatraz Island
Cabrillo National Monument
Castle Mountains National Monument
César E. Chávez National Monument
Channel Islands National Park
Death Valley National Park
Devils Postpile National Monument
Eugene O'Neill National Historic Site
Fort Point National Historic Site
Golden Gate National Recreation Area
John Muir National Historic Site
Joshua Tree National Park
Lassen Volcanic National Park
Lava Beds National Monument
Manzanar National Historic Site
Mojave National Preserve
Muir Woods National Monument
Pinnacles National Park
Point Reyes National Seashore
Port Chicago Naval Magazine National Memorial
Presidio of San Francisco
Redwood National and State Parks
Rosie the Riveter WWII Home Front National
    Historic Park
San Francisco Maritime National Historic Park
Santa Monica Mountains National Recreation Area
Sequoia and Kings Canyon National Parks
Tule Lake National Monument
Whiskeytown National Recreation Area
Yosemite National Park

The Hiker's Index

Celebrating the Scenic, Sublime and Sensational Points of Interest in California's National Parks

State with the most National Parks

California, with 9

Largest National Park in Contiguous U.S.

Death Valley with 3.3 million acres

Third Largest National Park in Contiguous U.S.

Mojave National Preserve

Foggiest Place on the West Coast

Point Reyes Lighthouse, Point Reyes National Seashore

World's Tallest Tree

A 379.7-foot high coast redwood named Hyperion in Redwood National Park

World's Largest Tree

General Sherman Tree, 275 feet tall, with a base circumference of 102 feet, growing in the Giant Forest Area of Sequoia National Park

World's Largest-In-Diameter Tree

General Grant Tree, dubbed "the nation's Christmas tree," more than 40 feet in diameter at its base, growing in Kings Canyon National Park.

Largest Elephant Seal Population on Earth

San Miguel Island, Channel Islands National Park

Highest Point in Contiguous U.S.

Mt. Whitney (14,508 feet in elevation) on the far eastern boundary of Sequoia National Park

Lowest Point in Western Hemisphere

Badwater (282 feet below sea level) in Death Valley National Park

California's Largest Island

Santa Cruz Island, Channel Islands National Park

Only Major Metropolis Bisected by a Mountain Range

Los Angeles, by the Santa Monica Mountains (National Recreation Area)

Highest Waterfall in North America

Yosemite Falls, at 2,425 feet, in Yosemite National Park

CHUCK GRAHAM

Chuck Graham is a freelance writer and photographer based in Carpinteria, California. A longtime City of Carpinteria lifeguard, Chuck has led kayak tours at Channel Islands National Park for 20 years. His work has been published in *Backpacker, BBC Wildlife Magazine, National Geographic for Kids, National Geographic Books, Canoe & Kayak, Men's Journal, Outdoor Photographer, Natural History, American Forests* and *Westways*. He pens the column "Unpredictable Wilderness" for the Coastal View News in Carpinteria. His award-winning book, *Carrizo Plain, Where the Mountains Meet the Grasslands*, was published in 2020. Learn more at chuckgrahamphoto.com. Instagram: @chuckgrahamphoto.

CHUCK GRAHAM:
"HIKE ON!"

JOHN MCKINNEY

John McKinney is an award-winning writer, public speaker, and author of 30 hiking-themed books: inspiring narratives, top-selling guides, books for children.

John is particularly passionate about sharing the stories of California trails. He is the only one to have visited—and written about—all 280 California State Parks. John tells the story of his epic hike along the entire California coast in the critically acclaimed *Hiking on the Edge: Dreams, Schemes, and 1600 Miles on the California Coastal Trail.*

For 18 years John, aka The Trailmaster, wrote a weekly hiking column for the Los Angeles Times, and has hiked and enthusiastically told the story of more than 10 thousand miles of trail across California and around the world. His "Every Trail Tells a Story" series of guides highlight the very best hikes in California.

The intrepid Eagle Scout has written more than a thousand stories and opinion pieces about hiking, parklands, and our relationship with nature.

A passionate advocate for hiking and our need to reconnect with nature, John is a frequent public speaker, and shares his tales on radio, on video, and online.

JOHN MCKINNEY:
"EVERY TRAIL TELLS A STORY."

HIKE ON.

TheTrailmaster.com

Made in the USA
Columbia, SC
10 April 2022